DATE DUE			

THE MINISTRY OF RELIGIOUS EDUCATION

John T. Sisemore
Compiler

Broadman Press
Nashville, Tennessee

© Copyright 1978 • Broadman Press.

4232–20

ISBN: 0-8054-3220-5

Dewey Decimal Classification: 268

Subject heading: RELIGIOUS EDUCATION

Library of Congress Catalog Card Number: 78-50388

Printed in the United States of America

Contributors

Philip H. Briggs
Southwestern Baptist Theological Seminary
Fort Worth, Texas

Lucien E. Coleman, Jr.
Southern Baptist Theological Seminary
Louisville, Kentucky

C. Ewing Cooley
Metro Counseling Associates, Inc.
Arlington, Texas

Howard P. Colson
(formerly) Baptist Sunday School Board
Nashville, Tennessee

R. Clyde Hall
Baptist Sunday School Board
Nashville, Tennessee

Gail Linam
Calvary Baptist Church
Waco, Texas

Alva G. Parks
Southwestern Baptist Theological Seminary
Fort Worth, Texas

Harry M. Piland
Baptist Sunday School Board
Nashville, Tennessee

William J. Reynolds
Baptist Sunday School Board
Nashville, Tennessee

J. Kenneth Robinson
Meadows Baptist Church
Plano, Texas

John T. Sisemore
Baptist General Convention of Texas
Dallas, Texas

Jack D. Terry, Jr.
Southwestern Baptist Theological Seminary
Fort Worth, Texas

Carolyn Weatherford
Woman's Missionary Union
Birmingham, Alabama

Jimmye Winter
Woman's Missionary Union
Birmingham, Alabama

Preface

Religious education is the flowing stream of a vital Christianity. In fact, it is the headwater of all that is meaningful and significant in the Christian religion. Because this book has Southern Baptist churches as its frame of reference, it may be helpful to clarify the use of the adjective *religious* rather than *Christian* education. No person or groups of persons decreed this terminology. Only the need for clarity determined the use of these words. Baptists have always been strong proponents of education, both in the churches and in academic settings. Simply because academic settings were more prominent in the early development of Baptist education efforts, they were referred to as Christian education as opposed to secular education. As church programs of education developed, they were called *religious* education only to provide a designation that would differentiate between the two educational settings. Actually, either term, *Christian* or *religious,* could be used to describe education at the church building or on the campus. The same term could even apply to both situations.

Even though a few persons have made an effort to create a significant conceptual, biblical, or theological difference in the terms *religious education* and *Christian education,* no such difference exists. The whole matter is simply pragmatism at work in communication. When Southern Baptists say *Christian education,* they understand that the reference is to the academic situation. When they say *religious education,* they know that the local church program of education is in focus.

Southern Baptist religious education is quite similar in many ways to that of other denominations, but it is highly individualistic and divergent in other ways. This book was prepared by Southern Baptist educators who are recognized practitioners of their art. It is committed to the quintessence of the Southern Baptist school of thought and practice. Its target audience is threefold: (1) the *academic community* and its concerns of philosophy and theory; (2) the *agencies* of the Southern Baptist Convention and their concerns for church educational programs; and (3) the *specialists* in the education ministry and their particular concerns for specific areas of religious education, especially in the local churches.

Because of the unique Baptist characteristics of independence, interdependence, and voluntary cooperation, it is impossible for any individual or group to speak officially for Southern Baptists. This book, therefore, is not to be considered as an official proclamation of the Southern Baptist Convention. It is, however, definitely representative of the assignments of the Southern Baptist Convention. It is written by some of the most highly regarded religious educators in the denomination. It was planned and prepared by the prestigious Southwestern Baptist Religious Education Association. And it is published by Broadman Press, an arm of the Convention's Sunday School Board. If "guilt by association" can be established by logic, then authentication is at least implied in the origins of this work.

The Ministry of Religious Education is dedicated to two groups of persons: one, those rugged and determined pioneers who hammered out the early developments; and second, those young emigrants who are just starting their educational pilgrimage.

The compiler is deeply indebted to the officers of the association; the experts who were co-opted in the planning stages; the writers who worked so diligently; Hazel Rodgers, who assisted in the myriad details of making a cohesive book out of fifteen manuscripts; and Vicki Hillman, who typed and retyped the copy through the many stages of the editing process.

JOHN T. SISEMORE

Contents

Part I
The Foundations of
Religious Education

1. The Biblical Precedent

Howard P. Colson, former editorial secretary, Baptist Sunday School Board, Nashville, Tennessee

2. The Theological Foundation of Religious Education

Jack D. Terry, Jr., dean, School of Religious Education, Southwestern Baptist Theological Seminary, Fort Worth, Texas

3. The Search for a Learning Theory

C. Ewing Cooley, Metro Counseling Associates, Inc., Arlington, Texas

4. The Meaning of Teaching

Lucien E. Coleman, Jr., associate professor of religious education, Southern Baptist Theological Seminary, Louisville, Kentucky

1.
The Biblical Precedent

The Bible furnishes clear and abundant authority for a program of religious education. Definite and strong commands to teach are found in both testaments, together with practical patterns to be followed. If ever a program were justified by Scripture, religious education is that program. A similar claim can be made for a program of evangelism; but the fact is that in God's plan evangelism and education are allies, not competitors.

Significantly, each testament contains a key passage concerning the responsibility of God's people to educate. In the Old Testament the key passage is the Shema (Deut. 6:4–9), in which Israel is commanded to teach each oncoming generation the words of God's law (cf. Deut. 11:19).

In the New Testament the key passage is the Great Commission (Matt. 28:18–20). Jesus there not only directed his followers to make disciples and baptize them; he also charged them to teach the converts to observe all that he had commanded.

In this chapter we shall survey each testament to discover a precedent for today's program of religious education. We shall note both historical and didactic passages. In the case of the ancient Hebrews, as well as in the case of the first-century Christians, there was a divinely given message to be communicated and a divine urgency about its communication.

I. Old Testament Education

In the Hebrew Scriptures the major word for teaching or instruction is *torah*. Interestingly, that is also the word for law. It is derived from a verb meaning to point out, to show—hence, to give direction. Another later verb means to discipline, to correct, to admonish. Other Old Testament terms for education convey the ideas of discernment, wisdom, knowledge, illumination, vision, inspiration, and nourishment.

1. A Philosophy of Education

The Old Testament philosophy of education is effectively stated in Psalm 78:3–7. There God's people promise that they will faithfully teach each rising generation "the glorious deeds of the Lord" (v. 4, RSV).

Several references indicate that God himself is the real teacher (e.g., Isa. 30:20). His people are bidden to look to him and to his Word for instruction (Ps. 78:1; 119:27; Isa. 8:19–20; 54:13; Jer. 31:33–34). However, stress is laid on the fact that God uses men through whom to communicate his message (Deut. 5:1–5). God repeatedly is reported as having commanded and inspired men to teach.

2. Early Days

In patriarchal days there was no organized system of instruction. The home was the only school, and parents were the only teachers. But the instruction was real, the most important part of it being the transmission of the sacred traditions.

We can only speculate as to how faithful the Hebrews were in giving religious instruction to their children during the years of Egyptian slavery. However, it seems fair to assume that the child Moses was taught in his parental home something of the essentials of the primitive Hebrew faith.

In terms of the Mosaic legislation, we have already seen that the Shema commands the teaching of the Torah. The entire adult community carried this responsibility. They were to teach the faith to which they were committed, telling the story of what God had done for his people in the past. They were also to set forth what he expected of them and offered them in the present.

Deuteronomy 6 emphasizes persistence in teaching, the use of informal opportunities, the use of the home, and the responsibility of the father. The communication of the faith to the younger generation was so important that the Israelites were exhorted to converse on the subject not only at home but when walking on the road, at the close of the day, and at the beginning of the day. They were also to have symbols on their bodies and on the gates of their houses to remind every member of the family of God's commandments.

3. Aims and Methods

The aims of education were three: (1) transmission of the historical heritage (Ex. 12:26–27; 13:7–8,14; Deut. 4:9–10; 6:20–21; 7:6–19; 32:7); (2) instruction concerning the religious ceremonies; and (3) transmission of the ethical heritage (Ex. 20:1–17). Central in all was the fact that God had made a solemn covenant with his people; thus they were under solemn obligation to him. An effective teaching method was to arouse the child's curiosity and then answer his questions (Ex. 12:26–27; Josh. 4:21–22).

As we have said, parents carried the main responsibility as teachers. Every father, for example, was expected to explain to his son the origin and meaning of the Passover ceremony (Ex. 13:8). Although many Old Testament passages emphasize the teaching responsibility of the father, by the time the book of Proverbs appeared the mother, too, was recognized as a teacher in the home (Prov. 1:8; 6:20).

Children were held in high regard in ancient Israel (Pss. 127:3; 128:3–4; Job 5:25; Zech. 8:5). Naturally, therefore, their careful upbringing and education were very important functions.

The methods employed are both interesting and significant. Most instruction was oral. Memorization was of primary importance, and mnemonic devices were used. Another teaching method was the parable. A highly important part of Jewish education was the annual festivals, which dramatically celebrated the mighty acts of God on behalf of his people.

4. The Judges

During the period of the conquest and settlement of Canaan, the judges served as military leaders and settlers of disputes rather than as teachers. So the people, during that lawless and unsettled time, lacked greatly in educational leadership. However, Samuel, the last of the judges, was a significant exception to the rule. He, next to Moses, was the greatest religious teacher in early Israel.

5. The Sages

Later on, King Solomon became the representative of the wise men or sages. The climax of wisdom teaching belongs to the postexilic period, but the book of Proverbs had its beginning with Solomon. That book is the biblical repository of the experience, wisdom, and learning of the wise men. Next to the Torah, it is the oldest handbook of Hebrew education. The heart of its teachings is that the fear of the Lord is the beginning of wisdom. Proverbs is a guidebook for successful living (4:10,13,20–23; 8:35; 11:30; 12:28; 14:27). Its purpose is stated in 1:2–4.

6. Adult Education

Jewish education was not confined to children; adults needed education, too. It was the function of the priests and Levites, as guardians of the law, to instruct Israel (Lev. 10:11; Deut. 33:10). One interesting example is King Jehoshaphat's sending priests and Levites to travel throughout the land and teach the people (2 Chron. 17:7–9). Adult education became more prominent with the development of the ritual.

In Deuteronomy there is a commandment that every seven years at the feast of booths there should be a public reading of the law before all Israel (Deut. 31:10–13). That reading, of course, would be public adult education on a large scale. However, it is not known whether this command was carried out with any regularity.

7. The Prophets

The educational function of the prophets must not be overlooked. Such men as Elijah, Amos, and Isaiah were not only preachers, but also teachers who helped to put to the forefront in Hebrew thought the ideal of personal and civic righteousness. The prophets were sensitive to the religious and social conditions about them and did much to interpret and apply the faith to their own and succeeding generations.

8. The Synagogue

As noted at the outset, the home was the earliest Hebrew school; and it continued to have a primary place in Jewish education. But in later Jewish history, another type of educational institution arose—the synagogue. It probably came into existence during the Babylonian exile. The exile was unquestionably a national disaster, but it was not without compensating influences. The synagogue was one of its major outcomes. In exile the people found great value in a meeting place where they could gather with their fellow believers and renew their faith.

The primary function of the synagogue was the instruction of the people in the law (Torah). The weekly service was largely educational in nature; thus all Jews became students of the law. By the time of Jesus each synagogue had a school for children. Memorization was the main method employed, and the aim was to inculcate habits of strict ritualistic observance.

9. The Postexilic Period

During the postexilic period the prophets fell into the background, and the scribes increasingly took their place as religious leaders. Thus merely transmissive teaching displaced preaching. This, of course, was unfortunate, for the scribes, unlike the prophets, developed a narrow system of legalistic tradition—the thing that Jesus so vigorously condemned.

A few years before the exile, King Josiah had officially recognized and sanctioned the teachings of the prophets and the Deuteronomic legislation. So when the exiles went to Babylon, they took with them the Torah (book of the Law). From then on, the Torah constituted both the textbook and the program of religious education. When the exiles returned, the Torah strongly undergirded their theocratic government. And during the later postexilic period the writings of poets, lawgivers, prophets, and sages were brought together into one sacred collection of scrolls, which we know as the Old Testament canon.

In this period the teachers were not only the priests and Levites but also the wise men (sages) and scribes. The scribes were known as *sopherim*—literally, persons learned in the Scriptures. They not only copied the ancient writings, but they also interpreted them.

From Ezra's time onward, the Jews became known as "the people of the book." Ezra was both a priest and a *sopher* (wise man), of whom it is written that he "set his heart to study the law of the Lord, and to do it, and to teach his statutes and ordinances in Israel" (Ezra 7:10, RSV).

Under Ezra occurred the most striking Old Testament instance of public instruction in the Scriptures (Neh. 8). The spiritual, ceremonial, social, and civic effects were outstandingly significant (Neh. 9–10) and greatly influenced the future history of the Jews.

We have now seen that in the Old Testament, religious education, along with the preaching of the prophets, was one of the most significant responsibilities and far-reaching influences in the people's lives. We shall now turn to the New Testament, where a similar fact is found.

II. NEW TESTAMENT EDUCATION

In a very real sense, Old Testament education prepared the way for the teaching program of the New Testament. The Christian view of God is the outgrowth of the lofty monotheism of the Jews with its emphasis on righteousness and holiness of life. Jesus, in his teaching, not only made great use of the Hebrew Scriptures; but he also threw a flood of light on their deeper meaning.

1. Jesus the Master Teacher

Both by example and command Jesus emphasized the importance of the teaching ministry. He himself was preeminently a teacher— a teacher "come from God" (John 3:2). During his earthly mission he was called "Teacher" more often than by any other designation. In the four Gospels he is referred to as a teacher eighty-nine times; he is referred to as a preacher only twelve times. Of course, his teaching and preaching often merged, but his work of teaching was basic and central in all he did. The greatest school ever to exist consisted of Jesus as teacher and the twelve apostles as learners. He also taught great multitudes. His principles and methods constitute the ideal toward which all Christian educators should strive.

2. The Great Commission

Jesus intended that his church should be a teaching church. The religion he founded is a teaching religion. As already noted, this fact is explicit in the Great Commission, every part of which calls for a program of teaching and training.

In this program the making of disciples is the first step. The very word *disciple* means learner and therefore calls for an educational process. No better way of making disciples exists than teaching people the truth as it is found in Jesus.

The second step is baptizing disciples. Baptism itself is a visual aid in teaching the saving power of Christ's death, burial, and resurrection. This symbolic act needs to be interpreted and made clear to every baptismal candidate.

The final stage in the program of teaching and training is a continuing process—namely, teaching disciples to practice all that Jesus has commanded. This calls for a program involving every member of the church. Conversion and baptism are not the end of a process; rather, they are the beginning. Baptism must be followed by an ongoing program of education; otherwise, converts remain babes in Christ, and the consequences are serious—for them, for their church, and for the cause of Christ. We make a serious mistake if we assume that the Great Commission deals only with conversion. That is only the opening part of it.

Another point to be noted is that in the original language of Matthew 28:19, the word for "go" is a participle. So the correct, rather literal English rendering would be, "As you go, make disciples." That translation would seem to suggest that in our daily walk as Christians, as we go about our various other tasks, we are to seek to make disciples. This concept reminds us of the Shema, which instructed the Hebrews, as they walked by the way, to teach their children.

3. The Early Church and the Apostles

The disciples of Jesus perpetuated his teaching ministry. In line with the Great Commission, the New Testament church became a teaching-learning fellowship. Luke wrote that after the great ingathering at Pentecost, the members of the new community were continually devoting themselves to the instruction given by the apostles (Acts 2:42). Such instruction was essential if the converts were to be assimilated into the distinctive way of life that Christ had taught.

In those early days the apostles wisely employed the combination approach of evangelism and teaching, for we read of them that they "did not cease teaching and preaching Jesus as the Christ" (Acts 5:42, RSV).

Of necessity the missionary and evangelistic work of the apostolic church was educational in nature. During the highly important period, the work of the apostles, evangelists, and pastors, as well as professional teachers, had to include a great deal of systematic spiritual instruction. This was true whether the learners were Jewish, Gentile, or a mixture of both.

When the apostle Paul came to the fore as an exponent of the

Christian faith, he, like the other apostles, gave himself with diligent devotion to a teaching ministry. For example, he was teamed with Barnabas at Antioch in Syria for a whole year, teaching "a large company of people" (Acts 11:26, RSV). In Corinth "he stayed a year and six months, teaching the word of God among them" (Acts 18:11, RSV). At Ephesus he taught the disciples "in public and from house to house" (Acts 20:20, RSV). The last thing Luke told us about the great apostle refers to him as being in Rome, "preaching the word of God and teaching about the Lord Jesus Christ" (Acts 28:31, RSV). (See also Acts 15:35; 17:1–3,10–17; 19:8–10; 28:23). Furthermore, each of Paul's letters had, to a greater or lesser extent, a teaching purpose.

The apostles' teaching consisted of (1) the message they had received from Jesus—both religious and ethical—together with (2) their recollection of his life and work, and (3) their interpretation of his person in the light of the Old Testament Scriptures. In a word, what they taught was essentially the message found in the New Testament today.

4. The Place of the Scriptures

In this connection it is important to realize that most, if not all, of the books of the New Testament came into being for instructional purposes. The Gospel of Matthew, for example, was and is an excellent training manual for new Christians.

However, during the years before the books of the New Testament were written, the church already had a textbook for its educational ministry—the Old Testament Scriptures. In them, believers discovered Christ and found guidance in living their lives to his glory. It was of these Scriptures that Paul wrote: "All scripture is inspired by God and profitable for teaching, for reproof, for correction, and for training in righteousness, that the man of God may be complete, equipped for every good work" (2 Tim. 3:16–17, RSV). Thus the biblical precedent for a program of religious education calls for the use of both the Old and New Testament Scriptures as the divinely given textbook.

5. A Special Order in the Ministry

According to the New Testament, there is a special teaching order in the ministry. The early church thus had officials whose primary task was educational (Rom. 12:6–8; 1 Cor. 12:4–10,27–31; Eph. 4:11; 1 Tim. 3:1–13; Titus 1:7–9). Their purpose was to work with the Holy Spirit in producing (1) spiritual Christians (1 Cor. 2:14–16); (2) mature Christians (Eph. 4:13); and (3) loving Christians (1 Thess. 3:12).

Paul in 1 Corinthians 12:28 listed teachers next in order after prophets (preachers), although in Ephesians 4:11 he put evangelists and pastors ahead of them. Both passages, however, clearly indicate that teachers were an essential part of the early church's ministry. The ability to teach, Paul wrote, is a gift of the Holy Spirit (1 Cor. 12:8; Eph. 4:11; 1 Tim. 2:7; 2 Tim. 1:11). Accordingly, there is a very high regard for teaching throughout the New Testament.

In addition to the special group of teachers in the early church, every pastor was expected to be a teacher. And concerning the pastor-teacher, Paul wrote that "he must hold firm to the sure word as taught, so that he may be able to give instruction in sound doctrine and also to confute those who contradict it" (Titus 1:9, RSV). Paul's voice still echoes across the centuries: "What you have heard from me before many witnesses entrust to faithful men who will be able to teach others also" (2 Tim. 2:2, RSV).

6. The Place of the Average Christian

Before closing this summary of the New Testament precedent for a program of religious education, we need to look briefly at the educational function of the average Christian. As we have just noted, there is a special teaching order in the ministry. However, we must avoid making too strong the line of demarcation between *clergy* and *laity*. The fact is that in a real sense, the rank and file of Christian believers in New Testament times were teachers. Acts 8 states that at the time of the persecution that arose in connection with Stephen's martyrdom, the Christians "were all scattered . . .

except the apostles" (v. 1, RSV). And "those who were scattered went about preaching the word" (v. 4, RSV). If the average Christian in those days was a preacher, are we stretching the point to say that doubtless the average Christian was also a teacher?

7. Christian Parental Responsibility

We have earlier seen that the Old Testament lays great stress on the parents' responsibility for teaching their children. The New Testament also supports this responsibility. Paul wrote, "Fathers, do not provoke your children to anger, but bring them up in the discipline and instruction of the Lord" (Eph. 6:4, RSV).

CONCLUSION

More could be said about the work of teaching in the early church, but enough has been said for our present purpose. In light of the facts presented, it should now be clear that the Bible furnishes unmistakable precedent for a program of religious education in our day. But more than that—on the authority of the Lord Jesus Christ and the example of the early church, we have a solemn, God-given responsibility to devote ourselves to the most comprehensive and thoroughgoing program of Christian teaching and training that is possible for us to carry out with the Holy Spirit's help.

2.
The Theological Foundation of Religious Education

The religious education experience takes place in a particular kind of context, one which is initially educative but basically theological. This context is the Christian community such as an organized church, a *koinonia* or fellowship, which finds its allegiance in Jesus Christ and in the individual priesthood of the believer, who enjoys intimate relationships with the Creator and Redeemer. At the center of the religious education experience is a message, a mission, and a command to communicate. This communication takes place best when it is proffered within the Christian fellowship of love. It is educative to be sure, but it is couched in a strong theological foundation.

The strong theological dimension of the religious education experience cannot be minimized because it is the dimension which is at the heart of the equipping, maturing process. The more closely a learning community can approximate the true nature of a church, the more effective its ministry of equipping and maturing becomes. The initial theological construct of communicated gospel is the individual faith of believers rooted in that gospel with privilege and power to encounter the Creator at a level of personal priesthood and service. This service is expressed in terms of actions that find residence in the Christian community. It is actually the living out of a theology of faith which demonstrates itself in evangelism, social ministries, missions, Christian service, education, and worship. The teaching ministry of the church seeks to implement the ministries in and to the world.

In this theological construct the individual believer is affected and effective through a personal involvement with a personal God. He becomes the heart of the communication process. The effort to communicate emanates from a desire of faithfulness to a commandment of challenge and a position of responsibility. It centers in the basic thrust of the educative impetus and the theological imperative of reaching and teaching. The believer is at the apex of service when life demonstrates the fulfillment of the gospel's imperative.

When witnessing and nurturing, or equipping, become the dynamic imperatives of the church, the individual believer begins to realize the significant outcomes of his own experience toward Christian discipleship as well as a responsibility to lead others to become a part of the gospel's redeeming process. The person is enabled to work and witness with the meanings and values of the gospel as the basis for total relationships.

I. Biblical Theology: the Basic Directive for the Ministry of Religious Education

In the emphasis on the Christian community as the context through which communication of the gospel will flow, there must be strong theological imperatives upon which communication is based. Three doctrines are paramount in the biblical theology that provides the basic directive for the ministry of religious education.

1. The Doctrine of God

God discloses his basic likeness in the character and personality of man, his highest-order creature. God's very nature is reflected in his creature, man, although that reflection is often refracted and broken. This fact is the basic explanation of man's capacity to seek for God's self-disclosure and may begin to explain his search for significance, purpose, and meaning which may reside outside his own being. Man is a distinctive creature; he is clearly set apart with characteristics, capacities, freedoms, and attributes that belong to no other creature.

God has created man with a mind capable of the discovery of truth and reason. Man finds himself invited to think God's thoughts and imagine his wondrous works. In response to man's mental thinking, God reveals himself to his creation as truth while providing for the discovery of these truths. It is in this framework of discovery and self-disclosure that God provides opportunity for man to discover truth in all realms of physical and spiritual conceptions.

God has, likewise, provided his creature, man, a capacity to determine right from wrong. The provision in no way assures man's behavior; it does through God's self-disclosure of himself to man give a consistent model of righteousness whereby moral choices are affirmed. God shows himself to be righteous by endowing man with a sense of right and wrong and by providing a dependable content of morality through his truth. Most significant, however, is God's self-revelation as he provides man with the necessary power to live right.

There is a continuous action of God reaching out to man with little regard as to man's response to him. Man's continual search for a power or deity to whom he may give supreme devotion and loyalty is met by God's voluntary disclosure of himself as he constantly meets man on his own plane with a promise of a rich, fulfilled life. This persistent pursuit of man by God has been evident in his dealings with man in times past; and it comes to fullest completeness in the person of Jesus Christ. God's pursuit of man continues in unceasing lineage as it is expressed through service by individuals and groups who have come under the lordship and power of the sovereign God and who now give themselves to extending God's ministry and invitation to man everywhere.

Thus God is forever in the work and experiences of man. He is accessible to man in his despair and frustrations, in his inability to reach lofty heights, and in his inability to make correct and proper decisions. Moreover, man can have the presence and power of God in every circumstance. The resources of the sovereign God are immediately available to the individual who responds in love and faith to him. The slightest response of acceptance will open a vista of gifts from God that will comfort, provide, affirm, direct, enhance, and develop that response to satisfying fulfillment. The individual is confirmed by the experiences in the Christian community as the presence and power of God in all his sovereignty is demonstratable in the lives of the redeemed.

God speaks through the Scriptures to his created being. The message of the Bible literally demands the interface of man's nature with the self-disclosure of God through his Word. Man's eagerness to have direction for his existence is rooted in God's self-disclosure of himself through the Scriptures and ultimately through the person of Jesus Christ. The Christian community has the Bible as the source, which in the language of men actually delineates what man knows concerning his revelation and serves as the primary instrument through which God's redemptive purpose for man could be established.

Therefore, the fellowship of Christians has the potential for facilitating an encounter with God through the realization of man's need to hear the gospel and respond to the claims of that gospel. The church, the result of God's redemption of man, is bound and facilitated by God's spirit and the common bond of debt. A major role played by the church has to do with the "right handling" of the Scriptures as a redemptive offer to all men. God acting through his people in gathered educative groups and dispersed individual witness gives opportunity for response to the gospel. In the preaching and teaching ministries the church proclaims what God has done for man through his self-disclosure of himself in Jesus Christ. This aim of self-disclosure is toward all men. God's use of the church to reveal himself is not limited to corporate gatherings. But God makes himself known through words and actions of believers, led by the Spirit, as they live lives of obedience in all personal relationships.

2. The Doctrine of Man

When man becomes aware of his existence, he realizes initially that he is not the prime mover of who he is or what he is. His existence is not necessary in relation to the creative act of God— he just might *not* have been, had God deemed such. Man is eternally dependent upon his Creator for present and continued existence. Man comes to realize his creature nature in his experiences of dependency, which constantly remind him of his reliance upon a supreme being.

Man makes a second discovery that the existence provided him is a moral-social existence. The acceptance of this concept moves him to examine the personal center of individualism and at the same time the dynamic relationship of collectivism beyond the individual sphere. The whole human world reflects the personal-social responsibilities of man. The institution and convention preserved for the transmitting of being, truth, and value become a constant freedom or restraint for man.

Reactions can become individualistic or collectivistic, depending on man's interpersonal relationships. When there is no overt action against the individual or collection spheres, man gregariously groups together. However, within this strong collectivism there is a God-developed individuality as affirmed by the Christian faith which allows individual freedom within collective restraints. This practice is limited to a privileged, protected relationship commonly considered family or small circle of friends. Man discovers this privileged practice as he participates individually in the collective body of the self-disclosed body of Christ, the church. Within its limitations he can practice more effectively the moral-social, Christ-centered human existence.

A third discovery that man faces is the search for the permanent in the process of change and flux. The imagination of man directs him to see that the potential of everything is only partially actualized, almost always refracted. His perception of the world is incomplete. This awareness assists in the development of man's religious concerns.

How can a person grasp reality when all representations of it are mixed with reality and unreality? There are two means whereby man resolves the frustrations between the changeless and change. He must come to the place through faith where he realizes that God is a transcendent being and is not affected by change. God is eternal and is not threatened by, nor subject to, change. Therefore, the person who participates with God in the eternal is not subject to the transitory character of experience, but is affirmed in the changelessness of God through faith and not by experience. Secondly, man's frustrations are laid aside when he realizes that God is actively working within change and thereby joins with man in the process of uniting change with the eternal reality upon which it rests. Man wants to participate responsibly with creation and therefore contributes to change as an active agent of the eternal.

3. The Doctrine of Salvation

By pouring himself into self-disclosure in Christ, God, the loving Father and Creator, created man for the purpose of love and fellowship. In return he intended that man would love and honor him. However, because man was created in the image of God with a free will and the propensity to act responsibly, he chose to rebel against God rather than to respond in love. Though the capacity to respond positively to God was his, man alienated himself from the promise and presence of a loving Father. Despite man's sin, God has sincerely sought to love and seek him. History demonstrates how God has acted in behalf of man with the idea of redeeming man. Because of this aggressive act of love toward man, there can be a reconciliation and a restoration to the former state of fellowship through the sacrificial offering of Christ at Calvary. This redemptive reconciliation allows man to fulfill the divine purpose of his life.

The divine act of God in Jesus Christ confronted man with an unavoidable decision. The nature of the decision affects present life situations as well as commitment and also affects continued affirmation of sonship. Although a number of human factors are present in the divine-human encounter, man is always free to make the choice. A negative response will assure continued separation and estrangement, which eventually result in death. However, an affirmation of repentance in faith and love affirms sonship, which includes forgiveness, acceptance, and mercy.

As this experience with the living Lord occurs, man becomes a new creation in Christ Jesus. The fullness of a sonship pilgrimage begins and issues in the progressive discovery of all that God is and how he will be disclosed through the power and presence of the Holy Spirit. There is a new, unabridged completeness which is promised with God and revealed in Jesus Christ. A new sense of obedience to the Christ principle is discovered, and a new freedom to perform within that principle is provided in the lordship of Christ. Acceptance of Jesus Christ is the acceptance of a new nature which is life-changing and God-ward directed.

The continuing personal relationship with Christ after conversion is a spiritual maturation process. This process is fostered through individual obedience and discipline and through active participation in the ongoing existence of the gathered and dispersed Christian community, the church. The growth process in Christ is not automatic but is best described as a continuing pilgrimage. There are relationships with God and with fellow believers that must be cultivated. Although believers come from many and diversified backgrounds and cultures, there is a sense of sameness in the Christian community that gives life to collective and individual experiences in the more abundant life that Christ promised. The most blessed privilege, however, is that the believer finds that his growing experience with God, Christ, and the Christian community satisfies the most passionate longings of his soul.

One of the most necessary activities of a son of God is to develop a significant affiliation with fellow believers in the Christian community. There is no way a believer can live in isolation from other believers and remain a normal, growing believer. Some of his most meaningful relationships will be experienced because he has association with other sons of God. The believer, by virtue of his conversion experience, is a member of the family of God. A cardinal value of the Christian community is that it assists the new believer in beginning to recognize and participate more fully in the implications of this new relationship.

Though the Christian community is a satisfying experience for the believer, there always exists a dissatisfaction with much of the transitory world and its existence. The promise of the future hope, both through the Word and through the experience of the death of fellow believers, produces an aggressive desire for an eternal relationship which is more significant than the earthly relationship. The answer to the dilemma lies in the affirmation of the conquest and triumph of the Lord of history over the present world and its degradation. The full impact of this promise is refracted and unclear presently; nevertheless, it never ceases to rest in God's divine purpose, operative in the course of history. The hope of eternal life and the triumph of God's kingdom provide assurance for the believer. To be an heir of God and a joint heir with Christ is to realize a relationship that is eternally significant. There is power in a conquering faith which will be consummated finally through the glorious hope. Though the believer does not know all the future or the full realization of that hope, he does have the calm assurance that he will be like Christ, for he shall see him as he is and live in perfect harmony and fellowship with him eternally.

II. Practical Theology: the Foundational Need of Christian Teaching

A theology that finds expression in life is both the goal and the foundational need in Christian teaching.

1. The Concept of Teaching as Practical Theology

The concept of teaching as practical theology subsumes that man is educable and that through the process of instruction by other believers, he has the promise of responding to the newly discovered vocation as a son of God. The matter of becoming a faithful son with a life-style that reflects the promises of God is a growth or maturation process. God's call to Christianity is no ordinary call;

it demands that a believer bring all of his being and potentialities under the will of God, fulfilling his stewardship in all life realms. The man who responds to God's call needs no other reason for growth than the imperative "Be ye mature even as I am mature." Rationally, this purpose alone provides the concept of teaching as practical theology.

The meaning and experience of discipleship can be developed in various aspects of practical theology. These variations present themselves to the believer in terms of moral responsibility, believer relationships, economic involvements, the purpose and reason for obedience, purposeful social implications, examinations of alternatives, and the acceptance of consequences. Through participation in these vitally necessary arenas, the conceptual fertile soil for instruction, the believer can interact with the realistic side of his newly acquired vocation and thereby practice a theology that is the heart and soul of living as a new creature and a son of God.

2. The Context of Teaching in the Local Church

The Christian tradition of instruction faces up to its lifelong human concern for achieving competence by receiving help and experience from other believers. Discipleship is the required instructional context of the local church. The disciple is to become just like his teacher. The teacher in turn is to entrust to the disciple the keeping and proclaiming of the message. The description of the Christian life as discipleship indicates a similar relationship to Jesus Christ. This relationship is learned through the guidance of the Holy Spirit and the committed instruction of faithful teachers.

The discipleship of modern Christianity is a definite relationship as a son directly to God through commitment to Jesus Christ as Savior and Lord. There is also a practical relationship of learning and obedience in a Christian community, a church. The church provides the discipline and support in the learning and obedience process so that the believer can affirm, refine, define, and clarify the purpose to which he has committed himself. The redefinition and clarification resulting from the instruction in the church assist the believer in harnessing his energies to issue in productive Christ-like actions. The disciple in relationship to his fellow believers is corrected by, and corrects, the Christian community of which he is a vital, living part.

The Christian community will provide the impetus for the continued growth of the disciple. The eagerness to search and listen to the profound truths of the Bible will be heightened through committed involvement with the Christian community. The encouraged practice of prayer, worship, and reflection so necessary for spiritual growth will be centered in the community and its relevant meetings. The Christian who truly seeks to be equipped will be appreciative of the mutual correction and restraint among believers in the community. Likewise, the community will provide responsible activities which will allow the individual believer to demonstrate the freedom of life in Christ. The context will provide private and public worship, study, devotions, witnessing to the gospel, understanding of the secular world, love for a lost world, and supportive activities for family, community, and national life.

3. The Commitment to Teaching the Christian Faith

The basic commitment of the Christian is a concern for the Christian faith in expanding and broadening the kingdom of God. The kingdom of God is a biblical representation which recognizes the sovereignty of God and interprets for the Christian the mode of conduct and life-style necessary for life within the kingdom. The utmost commitment which must be articulated to every disciple is the accepted realization that life must be guided by the purposes of the kingdom of God. The Christian must continually make decisions whether he will support, oppose, or accommodate himself to the existing order. At every turn the believer will be confronted with partial success and partial failure. Nevertheless, the kingdom promise through the church renews and reforms every Christian community. Through this process of renewal and reformation the church commits itself to the kingdom and, by losing its life, saves it.

The commitment to the kingdom is to instruct every believer to live in the kingdom of God through abiding in this present world. The acknowledgment of his spiritual citizenship gives witness to the reality of the kingdom and makes that reality more evident. God brought in the kingdom, and man is called to enter it and live as harmoniously as possible in that kingdom.

The entrance of the kingdom of God is demonstrated through the life and work of the committed disciple. The gathered believers through worship, study, offer of repentance, seeking of forgiveness, and praise and adoration are prepared to go back into their daily tasks with fresh commitment and resolution to live as followers of Christ. The church is the chief symbol of the kingdom. It lives by its discipleship through individually committed disciples who, by their words and deeds, continually open the way to saving truth through Christ. Instruction for commitment continues as the cornerstone of the Christian faith.

III. Personal Ministry: the Ultimate Evidence of Religious Education

The involvement of believers in advancing the ministry of Christ and the mission of his church is the ultimate evidence of effective religious education.

1. The Acceptance of Priesthood as a Cornerstone to Ministry

When a man accepts Christ, he enters into a new relationship with God which initiates a lifelong transformation process. Further, he trusts his entire being to God. Through the indwelling presence of the Holy Spirit, the believer knows that he is not totally transformed and that there are things in the life which are not as they should be. But he dares to trust God, who began this process in his life, to continue it through faithful disclosures in Jesus Christ.

A new person in Christ submits himself to a new kind of servitude, a priesthood servitude. He offers himself as servant and discovers a freedom which he has never known. As he becomes consciously aware of this freedom in his life, he begins to discover that there are duties and responsibilities in the newly found freedom which must be performed for Christ to men. Recognizing that the Lord "came not to be served but to serve" (Matt. 20:28, RSV), the believer discovers that the Lord of his life is actively at work in him in an effort to transform the part of society that he touches.

There is another discovery in this priesthood. The believer comes to understand that the new life given him is to be shared with persons about him and that in the sharing he fulfills his total potentiality as a son of God. He is free to live and serve his neighbor in total dedication. This service is a priestly function given him by Christ and develops his life more consistently as a son of God.

2. The Actualization of Man as Acceptance of Mission

The priesthood of the believer finds its highest potential in the church, which is organized for the purpose of the self-disclosure of Jesus Christ through active mission. The mission of the church presupposes education. The church's effective use of manpower for its mission impetus will take cognizance of the biblical doctrine of the priesthood of the believer and will assist each member in the discovery of opportunities for effective ministry.

The concept of the priesthood of the believer involves the right of each individual to appropriate the message of forgiveness of sin as proclaimed in the gospel and the equal responsibility to witness to others about the availability of salvation for them. It is a biblical fact that every part of the body of Christ has a distinctive function, and every Christian has a responsible work in the mission and life of the church. The discovery of what that work may be for each member is a task which the church should carefully identify. The church is organized so that a framework for maximum participation in the mission of the church is encouraged in the life of every member. This impetus assures the encouragement and actualization of man as he accepts the mission of the church and becomes an active participant in that mission.

3. The Advancement of Ministry by Every Believer

The major concern of a church is to teach in order to enrich lives and ultimately to equip the believer to advance its ministry in the world. Every member of the church has a responsible place in the total ministry of the church. The truth is that every Christian is a minister of Christ and in the concept of the priesthood of the believer is responsible for performing active, effective ministry in the interest of his Lord. The hope of the kingdom rests on the church, which places primary emphasis upon the exploration and discovery of people who are willing to shoulder the burden of a ministry task. The church must be careful to impart to its members vital insight into the meaning of mission and the need for personal involvement in that mission.

If the church is to fulfill its ministry, then every member must accept his responsibility as a minister of Christ and participate in training and guidance that the church offers to facilitate effective carrying on of the work. In the light of this fact, the church must carry on evaluative programs of effective ministry in order to re-study the various forms of ministry. These studies would yield information on the opportunity of opening new vistas of ministry for individuals and groups. As the church offers these ministry opportunities and as members respond, it in turn blesses, strengthens, and affirms sonship and "family of God-ness." The family now becomes supportive, assisting each other in the world. The church then becomes, through its believers, an active participant in the kingdom which moves steadily toward the consummation of the faithful and the introduction of the kingdom of God in reality, not in metaphor.

3.
The Search for a Learning Theory

Teaching is not the same as learning. *Teaching* is what one person does to or for another. *Learning* is what a person does for himself—both with and without a teacher.

These three interrelated statements of principle are the foundation of a learning theory. Because the statements bring into sharp focus the difference between teaching and learning, they imply that a theory of learning is not only important in religious education, but is in fact imperative.

Because there are many definitions of learning, there are numerous approaches to formalizing a learning theory. All of these theories have significance, but they cannot be arbitrarily superimposed on religious education. The reason is obvious: The objectives, conditions, and processes in secular education and religious education are quite different. Therefore, the stating of a suitable learning theory for religious education is still very difficult, in spite of the many previous efforts that have been made.

A valid learning theory requires some essential qualities. For example, a learning theory should describe how persons change as a result of learning experiences. Also, a learning theory should indicate how a teacher attempts to influence or stimulate change in another person. Likewise, a good theory is one that can to some degree predict the behavioral changes caused by learning. A complete theory must explain why a sometimes successful teaching-learning activity that works well with some teachers and some learners does not work well with other teachers and learners.

It is obvious that many people do not learn even in a religious education activity, and it is just as obvious that many of these non-learners are eventually lost to the church. Why? Is it because the learning theory on which the teaching is based is not clear enough to include appropriate experiences for all the learners? Do we not need a wide-based learning theory that takes these matters into account, a theory that has theological integrity and psychological adequacy? Presentation and interpretation of such a theory is the hazardous challenge that is the intent of this chapter.

I. LEARNING THEORY REFLECTS ONE'S CONCEPT OF HUMAN NATURE

What a person thinks about human nature is closely related to his theory of learning. For example, teachers who overemphasize the fall of man and his evil nature to the exclusion of his spiritual potential will probably look for their theory *outside* of the individual. In a theory viewed from this perspective, various aspects of the learning environment and community will be highlighted. The authority of the teacher and the content of the curriculum will be seen as important in controlling the learner and in "forcing" learning.

On the other hand, teachers who strongly emphasize the nature of man as created in the image of God, even while confirming man's humanity, will search for a theory of learning *inside* the learner. They will want to discover how the spark of the divine image can be ignited. Their theory of learning will be concerned with the potential of human nature in a Christian context. Learning will be seen as a process by which the image of God can become actualized in human behavior. From this perspective, learning how to make moral choices will be an important part of the learning process.

II. LEARNING THEORY DESCRIBES HOW LEARNING OCCURS

A search for a suitable theory of learning should focus on the learner himself. If we can identify the ways successful learners learn, we may be able to state some basic principles on which a theory of religious education can be based.

1. Learning Is a Natural Process of Growth

No one ever asks how a normal toddler is motivated to learn. When the basic needs for food, sleep, and shelter have been satisfied, all a small child needs for learning is a safe, protected place with new things in it. The natural process of development causes learning. It is essentially automatic because growth motivates learning.

Some of the natural process of growth remains throughout life, and even in advanced age the developmental process stimulates learning. Only a brief self-examination will reveal the residue of the "natural learner" in every normal person.

The following activity will illustrate what the natural child has learned about learning. First, ask the learner of any age to draw a person. Then notice the lines as they are drawn. These lines will express what has been discovered about people, including self.

The preschooler and the natural child remaining in most adults will begin with a circle. A circle is the first form used to communicate what has been learned. The circle symbolizes a whole that is removed and set apart from the remainder of the world. This whole or complete self is inside, and everything else is outside. The self is inside the circle, cut off and isolated from everything else.

2. Learning Depends on the Right Use of the Senses

After the young child has discovered that he is a separate "circle self" and that he can hide inside, he also discovers how he can get outside his circle. The first things that are added to the circle-person-self are eyes. Then a mouth may be added. Most natural world explorers will also put ears and a nose on their person. These additions are the important parts of self for a learner. The senses are used to acquire knowledge and to facilitate learning.

A good learner has good senses. Seeing, hearing, tasting, and smelling are the basic inputs for knowing. The natural child is aware of the role of the senses. Sophisticated adults may sometimes forget that "good sense" is learned through good senses. Adults tend to lose some of the functions of their senses when they spend too much time inside their circle self. People who think too much and talk too much often do not see, hear, taste, or smell as keenly as others who keep their senses trained. To be sensitive actually means that a lot of information comes into the circle through the senses.

The search for a theory of learning must begin with the sensory learner. The first and basic way that one learns is through the senses. Students of language will recognize the connection between words for sensing and words for knowing. The word for "I know" may be the same as "I hear" or "I see." An idiom of English allows even the blind to say "I see."

3. Learning Involves the Use of the Muscles

After the senses, the next thing that the natural learner (child) adds to the circle self is arms and legs. The thinking adult may put a body on first. But the learning child is more functional. The arms and legs go directly on the circle. Legs are necessary to move the circle-person to the things that the eyes see and the ears hear. Arms are used to feel and move. The child is learning with muscles.

A lot of what the natural child knows is in the muscles. The child knows what to do. He knows how to respond. Using muscles to do something is an important way of knowing and learning. The relationship between sensing and doing is a basic link in learning. Knowing what to do is perhaps the ultimate aim of education. "Activity learning" is learning by doing.

Everything that we know cannot be put into words to be communicated and shared. There are many responses that people learn to make that remain unconscious. In fact, the unconscious has been defined as those things that have been learned but have not yet been put into words. A few adults and a very few older children have matured and developed the capacity to learn with their abstract thoughts. These people can read words and think and learn without ever experiencing with their senses, their muscles, or their imagination. Many of us are not mature learners. Until abstract thought has developed, there must be sensing and responding for learning to occur. When the actual activity is not possible, then the experience must be simulated.

4. Learning Makes Use of the Imagination

The imagination is a powerful tool for learning. Like any powerful thing, it is also dangerous. The story of the tower of Babel (Gen. 11) tells about the misuse of the imagination. The calf made from gold (Ex. 32) is but one example of the problems of human creativity from issuing undisciplined imagination. The imagination allows one to experience things that cannot be known with the senses. This development can be bad when people place faith in things that they have imagined but have not proven to be real. For example, some people in their imagination have seen themselves in flight like birds. Some have died when they tried to actually fly.

It is dangerous to trust unproven imaginations. But proven imaginations are the new creations and discoveries of a culture. Because of the dangers, efforts have always been made to control the imagination. Tradition and the scientific method are but two controls that become a part of learning theories. Both insist that the imaginations of the human mind be tested and proven before they are accepted as knowledge.

5. Learning May Come from the Experiences of Others

For the naive natural student, experiences for the senses and responses with the muscles are the best ways to learn. The use of the senses can store in the memory more information about the world of reality than words could ever place there. Some truth may not be known in any other way. The "doubting Thomases" can never fully know with any confidence unless they have had the experience themselves. But all truth cannot be known by direct individual experience.

There can be unpleasant consequences to learning from experience. It is not best to touch a hot stove to know that it burns. It is not even best to have another demonstrate that the same stove is hot by touching it. The easiest way to learn would be for the teacher to tell the learner that the stove is hot. The consequence could be explained, and the truth would be easy to learn. This kind of learning should be simple. It is not. The imagination should be able to translate the words of the teacher into a simulated experience that has meaning for the student.

6. Learning May Proceed Beyond Experience Through Reasoning

A complete theory of learning must include both the learners who trust others to provide knowledge and those who learn to reason for themselves. Reasoning is a mental experience that enables a person to expand knowledge beyond experience.

The ability to reason is generally learned from conversation with persons who have already developed the ability. The Greek word for *dialogue* is often translated as thought or reason. To "dialogue" is to talk something out with another who sees it differently. When that other person is internalized so that the individual can see both sides of an issue, the capacity for reason has developed. Reason or internal dialogue between two opposing positions is the ability to build experiences and to know things that the senses have not experienced.

Once the learner opens his mind to knowledge beyond his own experience, the complex problem of trust and faith becomes an important part of knowing. The faith learner must constantly decide if the experience of others is to be believed. The natural child learns to trust his experience and to have faith in some people. He is confident of the truths that are learned from self and from trusted others. In dialogue the maturing learner learns to accept some knowledge and to change the understanding of other data that seem to oppose accepted fact. It takes years of dialogue with others to be able to internalize the position of others and then to argue back and forth with self until the position is clarified and truth is reasoned from existing information.

7. Learning Is Closely Related to Mental Experience

People gain knowledge in several different ways. The human mind can be viewed as interacting layers of learning. The first or central layer is acquired through the personal use of senses and muscles. This is the only way the young child learns, and adults continue to add to this unconscious level of knowing. Then the older child adds a layer of information from the use of imagination. Later, language overlays a level of learning from the experiences of others through reading and conversation. Finally, a fully developed rational person is able to reason and literally to build new information from knowledge that already exists in the other layers of the mind.

Learning can and does occur in all of these levels of human mental experience. Unique patterns of individual learning develop from experience for each person. Some people remain as children and never grow beyond learning by personal sensing. This core level remains the largest learning channel for many adults. Adults who are exceptionally creative use their imagination for most of their learning. Faith-type learners must depend more on the experiences of others and learn by asking. The more mature adult will be able to learn most from his own rational abilities.

Life crises arise when conflicts in learning occur. An individual becomes a divided, fragmented self when knowledge obtained in one way contradicts other knowledge. These conflicts are resolved in some way by the individual. Each person learns to reduce conflicts in his own way. Some of these learned defenses against conflict-caused anxieties block much of the future growth of the person. This closed or blocked person has learned not to learn any more. It is possible to elaborate on this model to describe many types of learners. A complete statement of learning theory must define how each different learner learns. Further, it must describe how to predict the way a learner will learn in a specific situation.

The remainder of the chapter will attempt to describe how the theory of learning applies to specific age groups. It would be impossible to consider every type of learner at every age level. However, it must be remembered that if needs are not satisfied, they remain, regardless of the age increase of the person.

III. Learning Theory and the Preschool Child

The best teaching for the preschooler allows use of the senses, muscles, and imagination so that the young child may explore the world that is new and exciting to him. Preschoolers are learning how to learn. The small child who has already developed fears about life outside the small circle of self must be gently reopened and encouraged to look and touch and ask. These fears may result from either unpleasant traumatic explorations or from being punished too much for their exploring behaviors.

Learning to use words is the natural by-product goal of the preschooler. A child is not ready to read and write until words can be used for learning instead of experiences. If young children learn to trust others, then they will have faith in what others do and say. Without trust, a child cannot believe or learn from the words of others. A child cannot know faith until he has learned to trust; he cannot trust until he has lived with a trustable adult.

In religious education it is especially important that preschoolers have teachers whom they can learn to trust. The teachers must live the content of religious education in their relationships with the learners.

The words of a trusted adult alone are not enough to teach a young child. Along with the words there must be experiences for the senses and muscles. The good teacher will be able to note the difference in how a preschooler uses memorized meaningless words and words that bring to mind experience images. For example, young children can be told about people, things, and ideas that are abstract and unavailable to their senses and muscles. But to learn about these unseen and untouched things the preschooler must make a comparison to things that have been experienced.

By the process of comparison, the imagination begins to grow into the mature ability to reason and think beyond experience.

At first the imagination merely reproduces past events. This reproduction is memory. The skin remembers a soft touch. The eyes remember a beautiful sight. The ears recall a strange sound. All the senses and muscles provide memory images. When the young child learns to patch together several images, he may be able to imagine things that did not happen that way. Dreaming, like early thinking, distorts the memory of past experiences by blending images.

A person with a good imagination can break up old images and blend new ones with great creativity. While listening to a Bible story a child with permission to listen creatively will understand the story by personalizing from past experience. Slowly the child breaks off little pieces from his memory to piece together the new experience in his imagination. The child lives the story. This process is both learning and learning how to learn at the same time. In the preschool years, the learner is primarily learning to learn.

IV. Learning Theory and Children

The child who has begun to master the skills of learning can begin to gain knowledge through reading or listening to words alone. Previously words required memory or pictures to give them meaning. Around the ages of seven to nine, a great split begins to separate children who have learned to master words from children who must still use their senses and muscles to learn. The ones who have mastered words begin to explore with books and conversations those areas of life that have been previously unavailable to their senses. A new kind of excitement of growth and adventure motivates the word learner.

A wise teacher will not force the child still dependent on senses and muscles to compete with the child racing into the world of written words and dialogue. Much of the Bible is written in a way that activates the imagination of the reader. The Bible was written to provide understanding through the use of experiences common to the readers. Heavy emphasis on the universal symbolism of family and the pastoral life gave a guaranteed meaning to the imagery. But the modern child living in a small family in an urban area does not produce the correct image to translate the meaning of the passage. He has no background for doing so. Religious education must provide children with family and pastoral experiences that they can sense, respond to, and trust before the biblical imagery can be appreciated.

Once words alone provide learning, the child is ready to organize the world of learning. Rules and natural laws of physical reality are learned from the patterns of repeated experience. Children recognize and put these rules into their own language. These rules and laws could be taught with words, but one learns to appreciate or detest the laws through personal experience with them. For example, rules that guide the behavior of the child to goals and rewards seem good. Rules that bring failure or punishment seem bad. In the effort to learn, the fact of forgiveness must be experienced. The idea can be taught in words; the meaning must be experienced. To know the reality of forgiveness, one must have tried, failed, and been forgiven.

Religious education is a sheltered workshop. Conflicts result when one is taught how to respond but is afraid to try. Only protected practice with guaranteed forgiveness permits one to learn the new skills without unbearable shame from the unavoidable mistakes.

Thus in childhood, learning produces the skill of control.

V. Learning Theory and the Youth

The learning style of the mature child continues into the period of youth. But now much of the learning takes place away from the sheltered workshops of the home and the church. Conversation becomes an important part of the learning process with youth. Teachers have to listen to the experiences of young people before they can know many of the problems that need to be dealt with. Biblical principles must be translated into the experiences of youth.

This translation requires much conversation and sharing.

Youth conversation or dialogue is the way people practice making decisions and solving problems. In time a youth will be able to internalize the conversation and to provide both sides of the debate dialogue. The wise teacher will use his authority when and if youth accept it. But responsibility must gradually be shifted to the youth to make their own choices. Young people need a lot of practice in playing the game of "what if." In this way a choice can be made and used in the imagination, and the results evaluate. Dialogue is necessary to make certain that realistic results are thought out. Religious education for youth involves learning and applying a problem-solving process with basic biblical and moral principles used to determine behavior and to predict results. Adolescence is the crucial time to make religion work in daily life.

In youth, learning progresses to the control of imagination and thought.

VI. Learning Theory and the Adult

Good religious education for adults may include all the kinds of learning provided for younger age groups. Age does not guarantee growth in learning ability. Some adults can get information only through their own experiences. Words telling the experiences of others have little or no meaning for them.

Many adults are still trying to complete their growth through the developmental tasks of adolescence and youth. Sometime in their adult years many people who have delayed their adolescent rebellion begin to think for themselves. This is a time of personal inventory when one literally should make decisions to keep some parts of his personality and to change other parts. The continuing education of the adult is the constant self-analysis and development of personal potential.

Some adults prefer to remain like the uncomplicated child. The easier course for them is to ignore the complex aspects of life. Simple solutions are retained for simple issues. People who keep their learning simple always need authorities to give them information about complex issues. They must be told what to do. These trust learners ask for advice and depend on some authority for their knowledge. The minimum choice for the trust learner is who to accept for an authority.

If the search for a theory of learning found only trust learners to observe, then the solution for learning problems would be obvious and direct. The pressure for learning would fall on the teacher. The teacher's role would be to become active, and the learner to be the passive, accepting follower. But learning that happens with an active teacher and passive student does not really produce lasting results. The learner masters a few responses to gain the approval of the teacher. When the strength of the teacher is gone, the trust learner looks for someone else to depend on. A lot of instructional time is spent with a teacher being a support for the learner. This is not good education. The best learning produces a maturity change in behavior that the learner can control.

Not all adults want to learn by being passive and dependent. They want to learn to cope with life crises for themselves. The learner who wants to deal with complex issues will not be satisfied with the same learning experience that the teacher prepares for the trust learner. The teacher must always be present to interpret meaning for the trust learner. The independent learner wants to learn to understand his own experiences. Religious education for the independent learner provides biblical information and moral principles and teaches the learner to use them in personal decision making.

In the adult years the learner discovers how to understand what he has learned and is learning.

4.
The Meaning of Teaching

A parable of the mystic East tells about six blind men who went to "see" an elephant. The first man placed his hand on the elephant's broad side and exclaimed, "This beast is very much like a wall!" The second touched a tusk and said, "No, rather, the animal is like a spear." The third took hold of the long, swaying trunk and, of course, concluded that the elephant was like a huge snake. The fourth touched the rough, hard skin of the elephant's leg and insisted that the beast bore a remarkable resemblance to a tree. The fifth, letting both hands caress a huge ear, said to his brethren, "This elephant is like a fan." The sixth, grasping the tail, said, "All of you are mistaken; the animal is like a rope." The moral of this story is that each of the blind men had a piece of the truth; but none of them had the whole truth.

I. Conflicting Concepts of the Meaning of Teaching

The continuing effort among educators to arrive at a definition of teaching is not unlike the encounter between those six gentlemen and the elephant. Theorists and practitioners in education love to seize upon a single part of the anatomy of teaching and judge the whole by that one part.

Carl Rogers is a case in point. This distinguished psychologist astonished not a few readers when he stated bluntly: "Teaching is, for me, a relatively unimportant and vastly overvalued activity." But he based his case on restrictive dictionary definitions of teaching. He wrote: "Teaching means 'to instruct.' Personally I am not much interested in instructing another in what he should know or think. 'To impart knowledge or skill.' My reaction is, why not be more efficient, using a book or programmed learning? 'To make to know.' Here my hackles rise. I have no wish to *make* anyone know something. 'To show, guide, direct.' As I see it, too many people have been shown, guided, directed." [1]

So there you have it. So much for teaching. Having set up his straw man, Rogers handily knocked it over. But was he really talking about teaching? Or was he jousting with a narrow, pinched concept of teaching?

Having disparaged the notion of teaching, Rogers went on to embrace what he called the "facilitation of learning." And what, exactly, is "facilitation of learning"? It turns out to be what many of us thought all along was *teaching*. For, according to Rogers, the facilitator of learning establishes a learning climate, clarifies purposes, endeavors to organize and make available a wide range of resources for learning, and serves as a resource to be utilized by the learning group.

On the other hand, there is B. F. Skinner, who states with puristic rigor, "Teaching is simply the arrangement of contingencies of reinforcement." [2] Teaching, thus conceived, is a branch of scientific technology in which behavioral modification is both the method and the goal. Whereas Rogers would insist that the teacher ("facilitator") play a very nondirective role, Skinner would put the teacher ("educational technologist") firmly in control of the behavior-shaping process called learning.

Rogers and Skinner are but representative of the tendency among theorists to squeeze teaching into molds of their own choosing, to the exclusion of other interpretations. In this respect, educational theorists are not unlike practicing religious educators, who also succumb to the temptation to fix upon some favorite shibboleth and use it as an unvarying standard for defining teaching.

I am referring to clichés such as "telling isn't teaching," a saying which has gained an amazing degree of credibility through sheer repetition, though it finds little support in empirical data. Some research studies indicate that people do, in fact, learn things by being told. The disciples of Jesus learned in this fashion, according to the following account: "Seeing the crowds, he went up on the mountain, and when he sat down his disciples came to him. And he opened his mouth and taught them, saying . . ." (Matt. 5: 1–2, RSV). Is teaching by telling definitely out of style among modish religious educators? Or is the real intent to say that teaching only by telling places limitations on learning?

Some become champions of "experiential learning" (what learning is *not* experiential?) or "activity teaching" (which sometimes is more activity than teaching), while the more traditional-minded plod on under the banner "Give 'em content" (as though everyone were agreed on what *content* means).

We organize much of our talk about teaching around rigid polarities—lecture vs. nonlecture; inquiry vs. exposition; content-centered vs. person-centered; teaching as art vs. teaching as science; transmissive instruction vs. discovery learning. This tendency toward polarization restricts our thinking about teaching, pushing us into an "either-or" mentality. It makes us ask, "Is *real* teaching 'A' or 'B'?" And it reduces the likelihood that we will ask, "Could it not be both 'A' and 'B'?"

The point is not that religious educators should have no methodological preferences, nor that one instructional approach is "just as good as another." My thesis is that no single theory of teaching, no instructional model, is comprehensive enough to embrace all that teaching is. It is important, therefore, not to let methodological biases lure us into narrow-gauged definitions of teaching. We would do well to be eclectic in our thinking about instruction, reaching out to embrace whatever conceptions can bring insight to the whole enterprise of Christian teaching, rather than retreating into oversimplifications of a rich, complex process.

This same concern was expressed by N. L. Gage more than a decade ago when he wrote: "For 'teaching' is a misleading generic term; it covers too much. It falsely suggests a single, unitary phenomenon . . . 'teaching' embraces far too many kinds of process, of behavior, of activity to be the proper subject of a single theory." [3]

II. A Working Definition of Teaching

Some educators tend to bootleg methodological biases into definitions of teaching. Dictionary definitions of teaching—"to impart knowledge or skill" or "to show, guide, direct"—are laden with presuppositions concerning the way in which teaching should take place. Little wonder that Rogers was unenthusiastic about such statements.

Here is a prime example of a definition which smuggles in methodological presuppositions: "Teaching . . . (is) arrangement of the learning situation so that there are gaps or obstructions which a child's native urges will seek to overcome, guided by a consciousness of meanings." [4] The writer of this definition betrays a partiality to a problem-solving approach to teaching.

A bias-free definition of teaching must be comprehensive enough to include all kinds of teaching activities, yet definitive enough to exclude nonteaching activity. While this sounds easy enough, it involves some difficult questions. For example, if a teacher is making a poster to be used in conjunction with tomorrow's lesson, is that a teaching activity? Is a teacher actually teaching when taking records at the beginning of class, or arranging chairs in a department room prior to a session, or digging out the meaning of a difficult Bible passage in private lesson preparation?

I want to propose the following definition: *Teaching is a process in which a person engages in actions intended to help another person learn.* The words in this definition are chosen with care. The word *process* denotes dynamic interaction rather than a static collection of elements. *Person* is used in the singular, but is not intended to exclude situations in which there are two or more teachers (as in team teaching) or multiple learners. *Engages in actions* suggests that the initiative lies with the teacher and that teaching is an active role. *Intended* is a significant term in the definition. It implies that teaching is purposeful, goal-directed, and deliberate, not unintentional or accidental. *To help another person learn* suggests, first, that learning is the intended end result of teaching and, secondly, that the work of learning belongs to the learner. (That is to say, a teacher can't "learn" anybody.)

This definition is deliberately open-ended. It is meant to include all kinds of teacher activity which is consciously related to an attempt to guide or facilitate learning. Thus, what a teacher does to establish a social climate conducive to learning is as much a teaching activity as is the presentation of a lecture. Teaching also includes preparatory activities such as making visuals, preparing instructions for small study groups, and setting up interest centers. And it includes contacts with members outside of class sessions, so long as such contacts are consciously related to the learning process.

III. RELATIONSHIPS IN TEACHING AND LEARNING

Some educators take the position that teaching must be defined by its results. "If no one has learned," they say, "the teacher hasn't really taught." This idea was embraced by no less a personage than John Dewey, who insisted that teaching and learning should be likened to selling and buying. Just as selling cannot occur without buying, there can be no teaching without learning.

At first glance, this point of view seems logically convincing. And it places a healthy emphasis on the idea that teaching-learning is a two-sided process, with both teacher and learner participating actively. There are flaws in the argument, however.

For one thing, it fails to take into account the fact that teaching and learning, as well as selling and buying, are interactive processes, not merely end results. A customer may spend two hours or more dickering with a car salesman, only to go away without signing a sales contract. If the salesman has not been "selling" during those two hours, then what word shall we use to describe his activity? And suppose the customer shops around for a week or two, then comes back to close a deal with that salesman. Is it not possible that the earlier interaction between the two had something to do with that decision?

To apply the analogy to teaching, suppose a pupil spends two hours with a teacher in an instructional situation, then goes away without having consciously learned anything. If the teacher has not been teaching, what, then, has he been doing? And what if the learner develops some gestalt two weeks later which, he then realizes, is partially attributable to that earlier instructional experience? Having denied earlier that the teacher had taught, do we then, two weeks later, say that he was teaching after all?

Another problem with the "teaching takes place only when learning occurs" notion is that we cannot always certify that there is a cause-effect relationship between what the teacher does and what the pupil learns. Faced with convincing evidence that a pupil has learned something during a unit of study, we may conclude, "The teacher has truly taught!" But how can we be certain that the learning has occurred as a direct result of what the teacher has done? If we take the "no learning-no teaching" stance, we are obligated to answer this question before we can say whether teaching has occurred.

And what shall we say about the possibility that a teacher's activities in the classroom may produce learning that does not even remotely resemble what the teacher intended to accomplish? Suppose, for example, that a teacher's zealous efforts to produce rote learning of biblical material causes a pupil to develop a pronounced distaste for Sunday School. Beyond any doubt, learning has occurred. Shall we say, then, that the teacher has taught, even though the intended result of the lesson has not been achieved?

To insist that teaching has not happened unless learning has occurred is to engage in a kind of semantic nit-picking which is at odds with much of our everyday parlance. For example, we find it easy to say that a mechanic has been repairing a car all day, even if the car still does not run when he puts up his tools. We say that a physician has been engaged in healing, even though his patient doesn't recover. When we observe that a group of people have witnessed some event, we usually mean only that they were physically present, even though "witnessing," taken literally, involves knowledge of the event.

Philosopher Gilbert Ryle [5] has pointed out that we often fail to distinguish between *task* words and *achievement* words. In football, for example, *kicking* is a task word, and *scoring* is an achievement word. Yet it is commonly said that a player "kicked" a field goal. A problem is *solved* in a moment of insight, perhaps after hours of hard thinking; yet no one would think of challenging someone who says that he has spent the afternoon "solving a problem." *Learn* is an achievement word. But we think nothing of it when a student reports that he has spent the evening "learning" certain material when, really, it would be more accurate to say that he has been *studying* it.

Implicit in the notion that one has not taught unless someone has learned is the assumption that the infinitive "to teach" must be used exclusively as an achievement word. But it would seem just as reasonable to use "teach" as a task word, to refer to a teacher's instructional activities without reference to the final achievement of learning.

The definition of teaching as "a process in which a person engages in actions intended to help another person learn" implies that the intention of the teacher, not the performance of the learner, is the essential criterion by which teaching is distinguished from nonteaching. This is not to say that teaching may be described as *successful* without reference to learning. Qualifiers such as *good, effective,* or *successful* must be reserved for that teaching which results in desired learning.

While this point of view does not divorce the teacher from responsibility for learning outcomes, it does strongly imply that the learner must bear responsibility for his own learning or for his failure to learn. From an educational perspective, then, a teacher should not be held totally accountable for pupil learning achievement (or the lack of it). Theologically, this position is in harmony with the doctrine of individual accountability and freedom under God, or "soul competency," to use the old-fashioned term.

IV. TEACHING AND METHODS

Referring once again to the proposed definition, the phrase "actions intended to help another person learn" covers a lot of meth-odological ground. There are hundreds of ways to help persons learn. Teaching activities may range from the construction of a machine-based, self-instructional program to the cuddling of a small child in a Preschool department. They may result from a carefully designed teaching strategy or grow out of pure intuition.

In view of all the possibilities, what is the best methodological approach to teaching? May we never find an answer to that question! Because once we discover *the* best way to teach and lock in on a single instructional method, we immediately exclude many other viable possibilities.

There have been hundreds of experimental studies comparing one teaching method to another, and the evidence simply will not support a claim of unusual superiority for any particular approach. Approaches to teaching should vary for at least three reasons. First, the purposes of teaching differ from one situation to the other. A method designed to teach inductive reasoning is not necessarily the best way to develop self-awareness or group skills. Second, teachers differ. A teacher who likes to be in control of the classroom situation will likely be uncomfortable with a Rogerian nondirective teaching model. Third, learners differ. They differ not only in back-grounds and personal characteristics, but also in their approaches to learning. One person learns best through logical reasoning, an-other by gathering and processing information, while another learns most through active involvement in concrete experiences. To respond to all of the variables in teaching situations with a single methodological approach is comparable to repairing an auto-mobile with only one wrench in the tool box.

Inherent in these reasons is an important implication for the training of teachers in the church. The well-equipped teacher is one who is able to draw upon a variety of alternative teaching strategies rather than following the same routine each week with unswerving consistency. No standard teaching outline is adequate for all occasions, not even such serviceable formulas as the old reliable plan that follows:

> Create Learning Readiness
> Make Bible Study Purposeful
> Get Bible Truth into Life
> Encourage Further Study

This formula is one way to work out a strategy for Bible teaching; but it is not the only way. The desired outcome is the determining factor in selecting a teaching strategy.

There are times when the plan for teaching needs to be constructed on an entirely different conceptual base. For example, one of the perennial thorns-in-the-flesh for religious educators is the apparent lack of positive correlation between the study of propositional truths and actual changes in behavior. Members of Christian families periodically study Bible passages such as Ephesians 5:21 to 6:4; yet husbands and wives go on yelling at one another; sibling rivalry proceeds apace; fathers continue to infuriate their children; and teenagers obey their parents grudgingly, if at all.

Perhaps what is needed for family life education and other learning situations where behavioral change is crucial is a teaching model patterned after Albert Bandura's system of social learning. An important element in Bandura's system is role modeling, which provides living demonstrations of the kinds of behaviors which the learners are to acquire. And learners acquire new behaviors by practicing them under carefully structured conditions. (It is not inconsequential that Jesus himself relied heavily upon role modeling in his own teaching ministry.)

What I am advocating is something more than the mere utilization of several different methods. I am suggesting that a teacher should develop a differentiated repertory of basic teaching strategies, so as to be able to function effectively under changing circumstances and in light of varying needs.

V. Teaching as Calling

Christian teaching is something more than a weekly activity carried out between 9:30 and 10:45 on Sunday mornings. It is a calling to be lived out, not just an act to be performed.

In the New Testament (1 Cor. 12:28; Eph. 4:11) teaching is regarded as a spiritual gift to be used for the glory of God and the building up of the church, not as an occasional function to be picked up and put down at will. The emphasis is on *being* a teacher, not on "taking a class" or "teaching lessons."

Teaching is to a Christian teacher what skating is to an Olympic skater. An Olympic skater engages in the act of skating during a competition; but what the spectators see on such an occasion is just the tip of the iceberg. Underlying that brief routine on the ice is a massive program of training, conditioning, and rehearsal. The skater's daily schedule, eating and sleeping patterns, leisure activities, personal conversations, friendships, values, aspirations, and self-perceptions are all wrapped around her identity as a skater. She does not just "do skating." She *is* a *skater*. And the meaning of that statement reaches far beyond the ice rink.

Similarly, Christian teaching goes far beyond a specified set of actions carried out in a classroom. It is a special sense of identity, a set of relationships, a life-style centered in an urgent desire to see persons grow in Christ.

Mattie Holland was such a teacher. Although she never knew it, she herself was probably the most effective instructional medium ever used in her class. She taught such virtues as humility, servanthood, honesty, stewardship, and love by modeling them in her daily life. There was a tenant house just down the lane from where she lived. One family after another moved into that tenant house. They often came in spiritual darkness and left knowing Christ because this teacher could not bear to see neighbors hungry in body or in spirit. No one knows how many times she walked down that country lane, a dish of food in one hand and a gospel tract in the other. She delivered babies, sat through long nights with the sick, and shared her meager resources with the destitute.

She loved the Book which she taught. The Bible was her daily companion. She read the Scriptures not because doing so was her Christian duty, but because they were as much a source of nourishment as was the food on her table.

Mattie Holland no longer reads her Bible. Her eyesight has failed. But more than seventy years of Bible study and Sunday School teaching have left a rich deposit in her life—so much so that now, unable to read the Scriptures, she continues to live out biblical truth day by day in the nursing home where she now resides. She recently suffered two heart attacks. A broken hip has taken her to surgery twice. She moves about in her wheelchair only with the assistance of a nurse. Arteriosclerosis has taken its toll of her memory.

And yet Mrs. Holland is still a teacher. No longer able to lead study sessions, she is still a teacher. Much of her teaching is now one-on-one, as she counsels the lonely, comforts the broken-hearted, and introduces her roommates to Jesus Christ. Yet she does not settle for that. On a recent Mother's Day my wife and I visited her early in the morning. We did not stay as long as we had planned, however. For at nine o'clock her room started filling up with other patients. Blind, crippled, feeble, deaf—they came, just as they did every week. In a few minutes a young preacher came in, a Bible under his arm. It was time for Bible teaching again in Mattie Holland's class. She would not do the "teaching," but she *is* the teacher.

What is teaching? Teaching is a process—*a process in which a person engages in actions intended to help another person learn.*

Notes

1. Carl R. Rogers, *Freedom to Learn* (Columbus, Ohio: Charles E. Merrill Publishing Company, 1969), p. 103.

2. B. F. Skinner, *The Technology of Teaching* (New York: Appleton-Century-Crofts, 1968), p. 5.

3. N. L. Gage, *Theories of Learning and Instruction,* Sixty-third Yearbook of the National Society for the Study of Education, Part I (Chicago: University of Chicago Press, 1964), pp. 273–274.

4. John S. Brubacher, *Modern Philosophies of Education* (New York:

McGraw-Hill Book Company, Inc., 1939), p. 108.

5. Gilbert Ryle, *The Concept of Mind* (New York: Barnes and Noble, Inc., 1949), p. 149 f. (The writer is indebted to B. O. Smith for referring to Ryle's idea in his article "A Concept of Teaching," *Teacher's College Record* 61 (February 1960), no. 5, p. 232.

Part II
The Religious Education
Programs of a Church

1. The Bible Teaching Program
John T. Sisemore, director, Sunday School Division, Baptist General Convention of Texas, Dallas, Texas

2. The Church Training Program
R. Clyde Hall, supervisor, Youth Section, Church Training Department, Baptist Sunday School Board, Nashville, Tennessee

3. The Missions Program
Carolyn Weatherford, executive director, Woman's Missionary Union, Birmingham, Alabama

4. The Church Music Program
William J. Reynolds, secretary, Church Music Department, Baptist Sunday School Board, Nashville, Tennessee

1.
The Bible Teaching Program

Sunday School—Bible study—Bible teaching and learning—these are specific terms that are used to refer in part to the Bible Teaching program of a church. The word *part* is used because the term Bible Teaching program is a comprehensive title for the whole of the church's efforts to teach the Bible, both at the church location and beyond.

Actually the Bible Teaching program, as significant as it is, is also a part—a part of the religious education program of a church. Because of the unique position of the Bible in religious education, the Bible Teaching program is magnified rather than minimized when it is viewed in the context of the whole of religious education. This premise is based on the fact that every philosophy, organization, and educational practice must have a strong biblical base or it falls short of being *religious* education.

Southern Baptists as a denomination are a monument to the power of Bible teaching. For more than a century, Bible teaching has been used as the opening wedge in starting new churches, winning people to Christ, and developing an army of lay leaders. Although many things have contributed to the rapid growth of Southern Baptists, it is quite obvious that all of them have their roots in Bible study, Bible teaching, and Bible preaching. What title, therefore, could be more appropriate for the most forceful and far-reaching program of these churches than the Bible Teaching program?

At this time there is no effort in view and no real reason to expect one which would gather up the various parts of the Bible Teaching program into one single organizational name. The term "Bible Teaching program" is a functional title that pinpoints the tasks that are involved. It is a generic title that spotlights the base from which the total program emanates. In summary, the Bible Teaching program is the sum total of all that a church does to provide Bible study for the masses.

I. Sunday School: the Main-line Organization

The Bible Teaching program of a church finds its ongoing organizational expression in the Sunday School. This statement does not imply that the Sunday School and the Bible Teaching program are synonymous any more than the church and the Sunday School are identical. The fact is, however, that the Sunday School is a unique and highly effective organization that gives structure and stability to the Bible Teaching program.

In recent years the Sunday School has again enjoyed great acceptance from the general public. To some people, however, the Sunday School is still little more than an hour or so on Sunday morning in which "the lesson" is "brought" by the teacher (the mental image is a lay preacher). It is easy to find fault with such a school, but in no way should this carry-over from the early beginnings be despised or disparaged. Inadequate as it is, it represents the heritage out of which greatness has grown and is growing. Nevertheless, any satisfaction with this traditional view of Sunday School is unthinkable. The Sunday School has much more to offer the people and the churches.

1. How the Sunday School Relates to the Church

Up to this time no official definition of the Sunday School has been offered or promoted. Now may be the time to begin to define Sunday School more adequately. Here is a proposed start: *The Sunday School is an agency of a church designed to assist the church in carrying out the Great Commission in the local community by reaching the people, teaching them the Bible, winning them to Christ, and involving them in the life and work of the church.*

Notice the three basic characteristics of this definition:

The Sunday School has an earned relationship to the church.—The early Sunday School had no relation to the church. In fact, it was generally considered a competitor if not an enemy of the church. It was often openly accused of "desecrating the sabbath" by its activities. Unfortunately, the Sunday School was not created by the church; it sprang up as an independent movement. Gradually the church became "converted" to the value of the Sunday School, and the Sunday School was eventually "baptized" into the membership of the church! Even though there are a few churches that do not have a Sunday School, most churches today consider the Sunday School an absolute essential.

Although it took a long time to bring the Sunday School under church control and into a compatible relationship, this goal has been achieved. The most commonly accepted attitude today is that the Sunday School *is* the church organized to handle many important responsibilities.

The Sunday School has an assigned relationship to the church.—The Sunday School, as an agency of the church, does not determine its own program. The program structure of the Sunday School is always the prerogative of the church. It is the responsibility of the church to make program assignments. These assignments are either made by special action of the church or by common consent. Because the program assignments are church assignments, no individual has the right to ignore or change them without the explicit approval of the church.

At the request of the Southern Baptist Convention, the Sunday School Board has formalized the basic Sunday School activities into program task statements. The following task statements are taken from the official program design of *The Bible Teaching Program of a Church:* Teach the biblical revelation; reach persons for Christ and church membership; perform the functions of the church; provide and interpret information concerning the work of the church and denomination.

These statements are official only for the Sunday School Board. Churches cannot be required to accept them. However, the statements are quite generally accepted because their value is obvious, even though the language is a bit technical.

The Sunday School has an interdependent relationship to the church.— As already indicated in the definition of the Sunday School and in the program task statements of the Sunday School Board, the Sunday School has a wide range of assignments. As a matter of emphasis it should be carefully noted that these assignments constitute the ideal expression of the very nature of a church; specific responses to the Great Commission; the framework of a stable structure for achievement; and the finest opportunity for Christians to discover and develop their gifts of the Spirit *(charisma)*.

Although the suggested definition magnifies the interdependent relationships between the school and the church, it needs to be reemphasized that the responsibility for the total success of the Sunday School rests on the church. In turn, the Sunday School plays the major role in the human progress and success of the church. *This interdependency is probably the most unique facet of the Southern Baptist concept of religious education.*

2. What the Sunday School Does for the Church

Both directly and indirectly the Sunday School makes many contributions to a church and to the kingdom of God.

The Sunday School engages its members and prospects in Bible study.— Religious educators do not need to be reminded that Bible teaching and learning are essential to the mission of a church and to the effectiveness of the Christian witness. However, it is important to remember that the kind of Bible *teaching* and the approach to Bible *study* in the Sunday School can and should be distinctive. Because of its unique nature and content, it cannot be taught like math, science, or Greek mythology. It must be taught differently. In fact, Bible teaching in the Sunday School should be different from the approach to *teaching, studying, and learning the Bible in any other setting.*

Teaching in the Sunday School should center on the biblical revelation. The term *biblical revelation* has three important implications for the Sunday School.

First, there is the *concept* of the biblical revelation (not to be confused or equated with the book of Revelation, although this book is included). The term biblical revelation is a distinctive phrase used by theologians to designate a special way in which the Bible is the *written* record of God's self-disclosure to man. It is this written record, rather than the revelation of God through nature or man's moral consciousness, that makes it possible for man to know God and to live in full fellowship with him.

Second, there is the *content* of the biblical revelation. In overview, the content is God's self-disclosure. From this viewpoint, the revelation finds its climax in Jesus Christ; and he is the master key to understanding the full meaning of the Bible. "When in former times God spoke to our forefathers, he spoke in fragmentary and varied fashion through the prophets. But in this the final age he has spoken to us in the Son, whom he has made heir to the whole universe and through whom he created all orders of existence" (Heb. 1:1-2, NEB).

The biblical revelation is therefore the good news of Jesus Christ. It is the gospel; it is the drama of redemption. This drama has five acts: the creation of the universe, the covenant with man, the Christ event, the continuum of the church, and the consummation of the age.

Third, there is the *curriculum* for the biblical revelation. Without question the entire word of God is for every person. However, the Bible is a large library of books that fit together conceptually, not chronologically. Also, the Bible is an adult book, and its material must be chosen and arranged to meet the learning needs and capacities of younger learners.

Although there are many ways to study the Bible, the arrangement of the study within the perspective of the biblical revelation best meets the spiritual needs of persons. Therefore, a curriculum which provides a comprehensive and whole view of the drama of redemption is essential. Such a curriculum will greatly aid in the kind of learning that moves toward that matchless goal "Till we all come in the unity of the faith, and of the knowledge of the Son of God, unto a perfect man, unto the measure of the stature of the fullness of Christ" (Eph. 4:13).

Biblical revelation also implies a special approach to teaching. It is an approach that is slanted toward helping persons come to know Jesus Christ as Savior and Lord and to grow in their capacity to be like him.

This approach is in contrast to a systematic, doctrinal, or theological approach. It varies considerably from the typical approach used in colleges and seminaries, where the emphasis is largely on the mastery of content and tools for study.

Teaching and studying the Bible within the framework of the biblical revelation is intended to be pragmatic rather than academic. It seeks to help persons handle the questions about life rather than develop theories about the hereafter. It is designed to give a comprehensive understanding of the Bible rather than an exhaustive knowledge of it. This approach to Bible teaching is designed to complement preaching, not to compete with it.

Because the Sunday School is a nonprofessional organization, it must not be assigned professional level responsibilities or evaluated from professional perspectives. It is an ordinary organization for ordinary people. It uses a common approach to a most uncommon challenge. It is a Bible study program *of* the people, *for* the people, *by* the people.

Obviously the quality of Bible teaching in the Sunday School is not all it should be or can become. Yet it is uniquely successful in doing what Christ himself began—communicating the drama of redemption to the masses. If the Sunday School is to continue to perform its unique role in providing Bible study for the masses, there are several problems that churches must acknowledge and handle. One problem is the current lack of strong conviction and commitment regarding the educational distinctives that have made

Southern Baptists the strong evangelical witness they are. Another is the weakness of commitment to Bible study. A third problem is the system of priorities that a church establishes which does not allow adequate time for group planning for Bible study.

Because these problems are more general than isolated and because in their solution lies the continuing vitality of Bible study in the Sunday School, it seems wise to treat them briefly at this point.

First, the lack of commitment regarding Baptist educational objectives and methodology is finding expression in many Southern Baptist churches. It surfaces in an attitude that anything in curriculum or methodology is acceptable. The "anything" philosophy is characterized by trends which, among other things, include the use of "independent" curriculum materials that are not generally acceptable to Baptists in their doctrinal stance. For example, in non-Southern Baptist curricula there are frequent references to the universal church but an obvious lack of interest in a complete ecclesiology which magnifies the local church body. In these materials there is a strong emphasis on millenial theory but little concern for a balanced eschatology that portrays the kingdom of God in all its glory. Also in these materials there are continuing references to the conversion experience, but little attention is given to a total soteriology which magnifies Christian service and leadership. Furthermore, much of the teaching methodology in such materials, especially for children, is overly symbolic and "busywork" oriented. At the same time materials for adults are either archaic or "way out" in superimposing fanciful forms of interpretation.

Today's educators must rethink their convictions regarding curriculum materials and the educational objectives they inculcate. Open-mindedness is one thing, but compromise is another. "Anythingism" in Bible study curriculum and educational objectives can be disastrous. Probably a strong and abiding commitment to a balanced study of the Bible will be the next big battle that educators must fight. A major part of the struggle will be related to the appropriate use of the denomination's curriculum and teaching materials. Southern Baptist curricula may not be perfect, but they are not the cause of the lack of vitality in learning. The approaches these materials propose for planning, teaching preparation, and learning activities may not provide all the answers, but they are certainly in harmony with the best proven technology. The educational organization promoted for Southern Baptist Sunday Schools may still need some adjustments, but it is in the vanguard of progress.

Probably the greatest problem in Bible teaching arises from the system of priorities used by a church. Sunday School planning and teacher preparation have declined steadily since the concept of "everything on Wednesday evening" became popular. This approach seems to ignore the fact that time for planning and teacher improvement must have priority, or the total church program will suffer. The present decline in convictions, commitment, and educational excellence in Sunday School work seems directly correlated to the loss or sidetracking of the weekly workers' meeting in the churches. Therefore, the establishing, strengthening, and revitalization of the weekly workers' meeting is an imperative need in most churches. There is very little hope for any meaningful improvement in the quality of teaching and learning until the weekly meeting becomes a valid and vital priority of the educational staff, pastor, and church membership.

Another problem that Southern Baptist churches must solve is the weakness of commitment to Bible study. In some churches there are members, and even some teachers, who already have approved or would approve Sunday morning study of almost anything in addition to—or in place of—the Bible. Granted that there are other good things to study, there is still the compelling conclusion that they are not worth giving up the Sunday School time, or Bible study per se, to pursue. To substitute anything for life-centered Bible study is to cheat the members and to foster the eventual decline and decay of the church.

The Sunday School expresses the church's compassion for people.—It seems quite obvious that a church expresses its compassion for people in a variety of ways and through several organized approaches. However, it should be just as obvious that the Sunday School is the primary and foremost expression of a church's compassion and concern for people. It is the only organization for whom every person, regardless of condition, is a prospect. It is the only organization that can make every person in the community the responsibility of someone within its structure. It is the only organization that finds, enlists, prepares, and involves its leaders and members in a widening search for persons who are still unreached.

The word *outreach* was originally applied to Sunday School growth, but in recent years the term has become quite broad in both meaning and usage. However, outreach is still basically considered to be enrolling people and securing their attendance in Bible study.

The Sunday School achieves its outreach goal in several ways:

First, it teaches to stimulate compassion. Because the story of redemption is the organizing principle in the curriculum, both the content and teaching approaches must keep this frame of reference in sharp focus. Also, two overarching goals should always be uppermost in Sunday School work: to develop a concern for people and to influence people to respond to a compassionate Savior.

These goals do not imply that every lesson should be an evangelistic study or that every session should include an evangelistic appeal. They do imply that a warm, compassionate atmosphere should permeate every aspect of Bible study. When this atmosphere is present, teaching will reveal a compassionate heart, manifest a compassionate aim, and elicit a compassionate response.

Second, the Sunday School organizes to reach people. Because Sunday School attendance is a voluntary matter it becomes necessary for persons to want to attend and for leaders to develop the desire to attend. When more than one person is involved in any enterprise, it becomes necessary to have some type of organization. Because a Sunday School seeks to reach all persons for Bible study and because all leaders and most members are expected to reach out, an outreach organization is essential. These facts mean that every organizational unit in a Sunday School must have special persons leading in specific ways if outreach is to be effective.

Each Sunday School needs a general outreach director, outreach leaders for every department, and an outreach leader plus group leaders for each Adult class. Outreach visitors are needed in the younger Preschool and Cradle Roll departments and visiting teachers for Homebound departments.

If a Sunday School is to be effectively organized for reaching people, it must also have a planned program of outreach. The program must include regular and definite ways for locating persons who need to be reached. It must have a definite time and a definite plan for making personal contacts with unreached persons. The program should include a definite plan for assigning prospects and securing definite reports on outreach activities. A good outreach program will also provide definite recognition of those who work at outreach and the results they achieve.

The outreach organization is made up of volunteers. Most of these people will have to be trained and motivated to reach out. The pastor, staff, and Sunday School leaders all share in the responsibility for training and motivating the outreach personnel. It would be difficult to imagine a more important responsibility—or a more rewarding one.

Third, the Sunday School cultivates the unenlisted. The term *prospect cultivation* is not found in the Bible, but the idea is expressed throughout the New Testament. Jesus introduced the idea when he engaged in teaching, healing, and ministry activities that were designed to open the minds and hearts of the people he wanted to reach for personal faith in him. In one instance he organized thirty-five teams of two visitors each to go before him to cultivate the people in the towns where he intended to visit later.

Cultivation may be defined in this way: a definite continuing effort to win the confidence and friendship of a person so that a teaching and witnessing relationship may be established. Without this cultivation effort, multitudes of people will never be reached.

Cultivation may take a variety of directions. For example, in the area of *friendly acts,* such things as personal letters, invitations to social events, participation in recreational activities, and the sharing of appropriate books and periodicals would be included. In the category of *special remembrances,* activities such as sending greeting cards on birthdays, anniversaries, and special days; providing an appropriate welcome to a new baby; and acknowledging some special recognition that the prospect receives.

Curriculum materials may be used in cultivation by delivering the member's book and explaining the plan of study. Special publications such as *Open Windows, Home Life,* and *Mature Living* may also be used to interest and cultivate persons. *Personal ministries* during times of sickness, emergencies, crises, or death are useful tools for cultivation. The list grows longer as the desire to be a true minister of Christ begins to stir the fires of creativity.

Cultivation is by no means a "soft-sell" approach to reaching people, witnessing, or ministering. It is a good and often an essential approach to reaching persons who may never be reached in any other way.

Fourth, the Sunday School enrolls to improve relationships and involvement. The purpose in enrolling persons in Sunday School reaches far beyond the need for adequate information. It goes right to the heart of compassion. Enrolling persons is tantamount to saying, "We want you; we need you; you need us." To delay, hinder, or impede the enrollment process is in essence saying, "We don't want you; we don't need you; you aren't good enough for us."

Every educator knows the value of involvement in the education process. It is amazing how few Sunday School workers see enrollment as the key to involvement. A growing enrollment is generally an evidence of persons becoming involved in Bible study and in the life and work of the church. A declining enrollment generally means less involvement on the part of new people and, even worse, the persons already enrolled.

A concern for enrollment is not a craze for numbers; it is the beginning point in involvement. A concern for enrollment is not a statistical mania; it is the key to involvement. A concern for enrollment is not the final measure of Sunday School success; but it is the most practical approach to involvement.

The basic philosophy of enrolling anyone, anywhere, anytime he is willing is a fresh concept that is prompted by Christian love and compassion. This concept communicates the true spirit of what a Sunday School is all about. The practice of this philosophy will enable any Sunday School to reach more people more quickly because it gets directly to the heart of personal involvement.

Fifth, the Sunday School visits to improve its ministry. People are not required in any way to attend Sunday School. They come only when they want to attend. They want to attend only when they feel that they are getting more for their time by using it in Bible study than they would in any other way. Because most people who do not attend Sunday School have no idea of what it can mean, they need to be enlightened. Visitation becomes, therefore, the most essential part of the initiation, orientation, and continuation of the outreach process.

The values of visitation could be extolled endlessly. However, it is obviously the ultimate way to reach new people, keep the present enrollees attending, and help the visitors keep on growing. It is also the most effective way for teachers to learn the needs of members, to find fresh insights for teaching, and to evaluate the results of Bible study. And in these two areas lies the road to success in Sunday School attendance—helping people want to attend and giving them something worthwhile when they do attend.

The Sunday School wins church prospects to Christ and church membership.—The Sunday School has never been an evangelistic agency superimposed on a church. This kind of relationship would be theologically unacceptable and pragmatically unsound. However, in the past half-century or more the Sunday School has played the most significant role imaginable in evangelism. Statistical tables repeatedly show a very high correlation if not a causal connection between Sunday School outreach and evangelistic increase. This phenomenon does not occur simply because the gospel message is communicated primarily in the Sunday School. It does not occur just because the Sunday School is the major church program organization. It does not occur just because the Sunday School is a significant aspect of the Christian movement.

The Sunday School's contribution to evangelism grows out of its nature. It has essentially the same goals, the same interests, the same message, and the same spirit of mission as does the church as a whole.

The Sunday School also plays an important role in evangelism because of its functions. It channels the evangelistic concern and talents of the church members. It discovers people who are unsaved. It enrolls people who need a Christian influence. It teaches the way to salvation. It witnesses to those who have not accepted Christ. It nurtures those who have been saved. It involves its saved members in activities that generate evangelism. It conducts projects that stimulate professions of faith. It supports and undergirds the total church effort in evangelism. *Everything a Sunday School does is directly and deliberately geared to evangelism.*

In light of these many contributions to evangelism, three specific axioms form the basic philosophy out of which Southern Baptists approach evangelism: The Sunday School is the church's foremost *organized expression* of its commitment to evangelism; the Sunday School is the church's major *continuing approach* to implementing its concern for the lost; the Sunday School is the church's *primary channel* for teaching, witnessing to, and involving people in the evangelistic thrust of the church. Sunday School evangelistic success is by no means automatic. A great deal of intelligent planning, conscientious effort, and spiritual motivation must be given to its work of communicating the gospel through an organization of volunteer workers. From the human viewpoint, there is no way this volunteer organization could effectively do what it needs to do evangelistically. Yet it is made up of the same kind of people that the Lord selected to help him spread the gospel. Although there is much yet to be done, Sunday Schools generally are making an outstanding contribution to evangelism.

One of the great temptations that professional staff members have to face is to take the "easy" way in evangelism—that is, do it all alone or find and train a select few to be evangelists. Either approach is unbiblical and unthinkable. No church staff can do the evangelistic work for the church. Even if it could, that approach would be incompatible with the requirements of the Great Commission. When the Sunday School is used intelligently in evangelism, more people are brought to Christ and more Christians are involved in making disciples. The "more" approach is not only scriptural; it is also logical, practical, and successful.

Although there are many vital factors that contribute to evangelism, there are certain tangible approaches that can be measured and evaluated. In a recent research project made by The Sunday School Board of the Southern Baptist Convention, it was discovered that the churches reporting the highest evangelistic results had five factors in common. The factors are listed in a descending order of priority and with percentages for each item:

A prospect file—92.3 percent

A definite visitation program—89.7 percent

A new-member orientation plan—71.8 percent

A witness training program—60.3 percent

A bus outreach program—44.9 percent

With the exception of the important new member orientation plan, it is obvious that the bulk of the contributing factors to evangelism are by nature Sunday School responsibilities.

It should also be emphasized that *every one* of the leading evangelistic churches has a strong Sunday School outreach program. Other significant Sunday School efforts, such as an evangelistic note in Bible teaching, make a very distinctive contribution to evangelism —even though this type of assistance may not be statistically measurable.

It is becoming increasingly clear that Gaines S. Dobbins was truly prophetic when he said, "Where Bible teaching precedes, evangelism has its richest fruitage; where Bible teaching follows, it has its most permanent results."

In spite of the highly significant contributions of the Sunday School to evangelism, many churches win to Christ and baptize essentially the same number of people each year. Two factors seem to create this stagnant condition: Most unsaved people enrolled in the Sunday School have been saved or have dropped out; and most professions of faith are children of the present church members. These factors are signs of ingrown religion. The only hope for changing the situation is to begin an aggressive outreach effort to enlist in the Sunday School larger numbers of unsaved persons. Educators and pastors need to face the fact that a static evangelistic pattern is sure and certain evidence of an ineffective outreach program and probably a restrictive approach to Sunday School enrollment. The Sunday School must become the easiest organization in the world to join and the most difficult one to get out of!

The Sunday School involves its members in the life and work of the church.—This task of the Sunday School is popularly referred to as the "lead to" task. It is correctly concerned with leading church members to worship, witness, educate, minister, and apply Christian principles to life. The programs and methods for interpreting and accomplishing this far-ranging task are regularly found in Southern Baptist curricula and program publications.

Most Sunday Schools are not living up to their potential for involvement. At the present time half or more of the members in a typical church are not enrolled. Because there is a distinct correlation between the percentage of members enrolled in Sunday School and the success of the church in keeping its members active, this statistic is alarming. Can such a lack of involvement be traced to any specific circumstance? Perhaps so.

During the past quarter of a century churches have followed organizational trends in business which have been beamed toward streamlining the number of personnel. The result is that fewer people are being used in the organizational structure of the Sunday School. This development swells the ranks of "unemployed" church members. At the same time there has been a significant decline in the emphasis on leadership training. These two developments have contributed materially to the present backlog of unenrolled, uninvolved, untrained, uncommitted, and unproductive church members.

Experience has shown that the Sunday School, properly used, can effectively handle the challenge of leading the church members to learn and apply Bible truth to daily life. Therefore, its leaders bear an awesome responsibility for stimulating, involving, and guiding all church members in their pilgrimage toward Christian maturity.

The Sunday School communicates information concerning the work of the church and denomination.—Baptists have long held the two-fold conviction that all church work is a cooperative venture and that all members are equally responsible for knowing and responding to the work of the church and denomination. Here again the Sunday School, because it is in touch with the largest number of persons, bears the greatest responsibility for sharing all pertinent information with its members, as well as for securing their appropriate response.

This communication task of the Sunday School is not an unnecessary appendage or a burden to be borne. It is inherent in the Bible teaching task, and the response of the members is an expected natural outgrowth of their Bible study.

II. The Bible Teaching Ministries

The Bible Teaching program is capable of providing a broad base of Bible study for the masses of people not presently involved. In addition to the millions of "typical" persons who are not enrolled, there are many atypical groups that have special needs. If they are to be reached for Bible study, unusual consideration and generally special organizational provision are necessary.

1. Provide for Persons Who Cannot Attend on Sunday Morning

Many churches, if not all, have members who are unable to attend Sunday School because of health, advanced age, family illness, and other valid reasons. Some of these persons can attend at a time other than Sunday; therefore, appropriate opportunities for Bible study should be planned for these persons. A homebound ministry related to the existing classes or a Homebound department may be used to provide Bible study for persons who cannot attend. In many cases a conference call telephone hookup can be used effectively in an actual teaching situation for persons who cannot attend. With this arrangement these people can be a part of the ongoing Bible Teaching program.

2. Create Special Units for Persons Who Speak Spanish

There are many Spanish-speaking persons all over the nation. Most of these persons speak or understand English only with great difficulty. However, many of them are very responsive to Bible study, especially if classes are conducted in Spanish.

A number of approaches are effective in reaching persons of Hispanic origin. For example, a class in Spanish for older persons and/or for young children may be provided. An entire Spanish department is possible in many areas, while in some situations a Spanish-speaking Sunday School is possible. Such a Sunday School may be conducted at the sponsoring church on a flip-flop arrangement or in a separate building. In a high-density Hispanic community a mission Sunday School may be the best arrangement. All churches can reach some of the Spanish-speaking people in the regular program of the Sunday School. It is a beautiful thing to see persons of different cultures studying the Bible together.

3. Include Other Language Groups and Internationals

Pockets of people who cluster together for cultural and language reasons can be reached for Bible study when appropriate classes are provided.

Special classes or departments for a mixed group of internationals are often very effective in reaching out to "make disciples of all nations" (Matt. 28:19, NIV). A class in simple English is often the best approach for an international setting.

4. Involve Persons Who Are Partially Sighted or Blind

In most cases the near blind or blind prefer to be in classes or departments with others who have the same problems. Curriculum matters and teaching approaches can be much better handled in separate provision.

5. Welcome Persons Who Are Physically Handicapped

Physically handicapped persons need special attention on a personal basis. Most of them prefer to be in the regular departments and classes and do not want to be grouped together or isolated. Their physical situation will be the primary criterion in providing adequate facilities for Bible study.

6. Prepare for Persons Who Are Partially Deaf

In most churches persons with audio problems will be cared for in the regular departments. Hearing aids of various types may be provided, and a "signer" may be necessary in many churches. Where large numbers of persons with impaired hearing are available, special classes and departments should be provided on an age-level basis.

7. Care for Persons Who Are Retarded

Special provision for the retarded is usually the best approach, even when only a few of them are available. Unusual care and compassion are essential in providing for the special education needs of the retarded, but fortunately this kind of concern is amply rewarded.

III. The Bible Teaching Projects

The ongoing Sunday School activities are basic to the total Bible Teaching program. However, there are certain recurring and non-recurring projects which support and augment the regular activities of the Sunday School.

1. Vacation Bible School

For a half-century the Vacation Bible School has made a significant contribution to the biblical, missionary, ethical, and musical background of children and youth. In recent years it has become an all-age project as adults have joined in increasing numbers in the annual event.

The Vacation Bible School has also become an effective outreach tool in beginning new Sunday Schools, church-type missions, and churches.

2. January Bible Study

The original purpose of January Bible Study was to begin the new year with an in-depth Bible study. Such a period of concentrated Bible study has become increasingly popular, even though it is not always confined to a week in January. Probably more people are attracted to this Bible study activity than any other kind except Sunday School. In the beginning January Bible Study was for adults only, but it is now an all-age event.

3. Bible Study Courses

The Bible Survey Series, along with other Bible study books in the New Church Study Course, offers supplementary and complementary Bible study opportunities. Studies based on these books offer many possibilities for informal and even highly technical approaches to Bible study.

4. Bible Conferences

The Bible conference is a flexible and effective way to support the regular Sunday School Bible study curricula. Experience shows that such conferences produce the best results when they are appropriately integrated into the total Bible Teaching program of a church rather than conducted as a separate or oblique project. Bible conferences are also frequently offered on an associational basis.

5. Fellowship Bible Classes

Even though there may be church relationship and doctrinal problems generated by some Fellowship Bible Classes, these Bible study groups are effective when the purpose is geared to outreach. A church will need to exercise care in the selection of leaders and curriculum for these Bible classes. Church control is essential because the classes can be infiltrated by individuals having selfish or even ulterior motives, thus causing the classes to become ingrown parachurch groups rather than the outreach posts they are intended to be.

6. Dated Emphases

Rapid change in the world order creates many opportunities for the Sunday School to respond to current needs by projecting dated emphases. Probably these emphases would be most productive when they relate Bible truth to current issues, problems, or Christian opportunity in the world.

CONCLUSION

Bible study is essential to the very nature of the church. It is also necessary to the natural and spiritual growth of Christians. In childhood, Bible teaching is foundational. In youth, it is basic to stability. In the mature years, Bible study is supportive and assuring. Therefore, for the church and for all persons of all age groups, the Bible Teaching program has the potential for being the most valuable and productive of all church efforts. If this is the case, and it is, it deserves full priority. When priority is given and when the Bible is properly taught, it will return personal and corporate benefits beyond any conceivable measure.

2.
The Church Training Program

Equipping or training is a biblical mandate of the Christian church and should be one of the church's top priorities. Paul indicates in Ephesians 4:12 that the church is to equip the saints "for the work of ministry, for building up the body of Christ" (RSV). Each church is responsible for equipping its members for Christian living in today's world.

Church members are to be disciples or learners and should be ready to perform the personal task of disciplining. This task should be a major concern of today's Christian. The term disciple refers to a relationship, the relationship between Christ and his followers. In John 8:31–32 Jesus said, "If you continue in my word, you are truly my disciples, and you will know the truth, and the truth will make you free" (RSV).

But what is Christian discipleship? One definition is "the Christian's lifelong commitment to the person, teaching, and spirit of Jesus Christ. Life under Jesus' lordship involves progressive learning, growth in Christlikeness, implementation of biblical truth, and responsibility for sharing the Christian faith." [1] The Church Training program is designed to provide the climate, the structure, and the resources to help churches equip their members for effective Christian living.

I. How Did Church Training Originate?

The Church Training program is the second largest educational organization in Southern Baptist churches. It began in 1907 as a young people's organization. In 1918 The Sunday School Board established a Baptist Young People's Union Department. By 1929 the organization was graded, and curriculum and promotional materials were being published.

The name was changed to "Baptist Training Union" in 1934 because the organization included a program of training for all ages. In 1959 the Southern Baptist Convention instructed its boards, agencies, and institutions to define their programs. Following this Convention action, a study was made of the church and its basic tasks.

As a result of this study, the functions of a New Testament church were identified; and church tasks were formulated, grouped, and assigned to church programs of work. These programs were then assigned to the existing organizations of the church to be conducted on a continuing basis.

II. WHAT ARE THE TASKS OF THE CHURCH TRAINING PROGRAM?

The Church Training program is concerned with preparing "all God's people for the work of Christian service, in order to build up the body of Christ" (Eph. 4:12, TEV). Five basic church tasks form the structure of the training program. The first four tasks are primary responsibilities of the training program; the fifth is shared with all other church programs:

> Orient new church members.
> Train church members to perform the functions of the church.
> Train church leaders.
> Teach Christian theology, Christian ethics, Christian history, and church polity and organization.
> Provide and interpret information regarding the work of the church and denomination.

The Church Training program is distinctive in that it trains church members to perform their full responsibilities as members of their congregations. It is also responsible for providing foundational learning experiences for persons in the Preschool and Children's Divisions. No other denomination has an organization similar to the Church Training program in Southern Baptist churches. The provision of such a program means greater training opportunities for the members. Ideally, then, Southern Baptists have a unique approach to achieving their church tasks.

III. WHAT ARE THE BENEFITS OF THE CHURCH TRAINING PROGRAM?

Margaret Sharp in *Church Member Training Manual* listed several important benefits to be realized through the Church Training program. She included benefits to the church and to the individual.

1. Benefits to the Church

Every area of a church's life and work is strengthened as its members become stronger Christians and better-informed Baptists. Benefits to the church include the following: (1) It infuses the church with doctrinal conviction; (2) it conserves the results of evangelism; (3) it cultivates church fellowship; (4) it provides the church with informed members; (5) it provides participating members; (6) it develops skilled workmen; (7) it builds the Sunday evening church service.

2. Benefits to the Individual

Benefits to the church are also benefits to the church member. However, the Church Training program provides additional benefits for the member: (1) It helps the church member grow spiritually; (2) it helps the church member develop Christian skills; (3) it helps the church member live his faith; (4) it provides support and a sense of belonging; (5) it provides satisfaction and enjoyment.[2]

IV. WHAT TYPES OF TRAINING ARE OFFERED?

The focus groups for training are new church members, present church members, and church leaders. The needs of these groups determine the three types of training included in the Church Training program: new member orientation, church member training, and church leader training.

Each type of training is directly related to a church task which has been assigned to the Church Training program. The intent of the first and second tasks are self-evident in the statements used: Orient new church members; train church leaders. The third task has two facets: Train church members to perform the functions of the church; teach Christian theology, Christian ethics, Christian history, and church polity and organization.

V. What Does New Church Member Orientation Include?

A comprehensive answer to this question requires a look at several significant facets: its role in initial involvement of the member, its contributions to the church, and its scope.

1. New Church Member Orientation Focuses on the Entry into the Life of a Church

Southern Baptists are an evangelistic people, yet many members are lost from active service every year. "One out of every two persons on our church rolls is lost to kingdom service through his church. One out of every two persons bears a negative witness to the world as to the relevance of a vital church relationship. This loss of members to active church service faces Southern Baptists with one of the great challenges of this generation." [3]

To orient means to acquaint with the situation, to set in the right direction, to put into correct relationship. Such training serves as a link between the church's evangelistic thrust to win the lost and its educational thrust to help church members become mature and effective Christians.

2. New Church Member Orientation Makes Significant Contributions to a Church

To consider the contributions of new church member orientation is to heighten appreciation and deeper conviction about its need. First, new church member orientation can help to ensure a regenerate church membership. The lack of an experience of regeneration is considered to be one reason many persons are not involved in the life and work of their church. If this assumption is true, then a church is responsible for making an effort to see that each member understands the nature of the relationship he is entering. In addition, a church needs to understand the new member's previous experience in order to minister to him more effectively. An orientation program with careful counseling can help a church maintain a regenerate church membership.

Second, orientation for new church members can introduce them to a lifelong program of growth and service. Each new member needs to understand and accept the privileges and responsibilities of membership in the church. Conversion marks only the beginning of a Christian's life and discipleship. In addition to helping the new member reaffirm his Christian experience, the orientation program should help him dedicate himself to a lifelong program of growth and service.

Third, new member orientation can secure meaningful involvement of all new members in the life of their church. Each new member should begin immediately to become a growing part of the Christian fellowship he has joined. He should begin meaningful involvement in the life of the church both during and beyond the orientation period.

The best time to involve new church members in the life of their church and in an orientation program is immediately after they join. A new church member orientation program can help churches lead every new member toward meaningful involvement.

3. New Church Member Orientation Is Varied

The scope of new church member orientation may be defined in terms of the person involved, the content of the program, the activities, and the external relations.

"The persons included are (1) all new church members, both new Christians and transfers of all ages; (2) the leaders whom the church elects to serve its new members—namely, the pastor, orientation teacher, selected deacons, and the organizational leaders for the new member's age group; (3) the members who make up the church which the new members join.

"The content includes the following subjects: (1) the source and nature of the new life in Christ, (2) the nature and mission of the church, and (3) the opportunities for growth and service which the church provides and encourages.

"Activities which make up the orientation program are (1) instruction, (2) counseling, (3) guided reading, (4) guided participation, (5) family involvement, and (6) special program emphases, such as fellowship dinners, retreats, and other activities designed to promote the personal involvement of each new member in the life of the church.

"A fourth scope—defining factor—is external relations. New church member orientation is a task that a church assigns to its Church Training program. The Church Training program accomplishes this task in cooperation with the home and the other organizations within the church. Finally, the church and the denomination look to new church member orientation for the new member's basic preparation for participation in the church fellowship and its program for growth and service." [4]

VI. What Is Included in Church Member Training?

Church member training equips members to participate meaningfully in the life and work of the church in the world. It is the heart of a comprehensive, effective training program. It helps church members acquire the basic knowledge and understandings they need, and it also helps them to develop the Christian skills needed to effectively carry out the church functions.

1. Church Member Training Is Specialized

If church members are to grow in their faith and service, they need basic knowledge and understandings in Christian theology, Christian ethics, Christian history, and church polity and organization. There is a core of content in these areas that every church member should understand and be able to apply. To achieve this ideal there are two church member training tasks. One is in the area of study of specialized content; the other is the area of skill development.

Study areas.—The task of teaching Christian theology, Christian ethics, Christian history, and church polity and organization is designed to involve learners in the meaningful exploration of the realities of the Christian faith and life. "These areas are intended to help a person develop a valid system of beliefs about God in his relationship to man (Christian theology); to help him grow in Christian character and the ability to express and apply in a relationship with daily living (Christian ethics); to help him discover and appropriate meanings and values in Christian history; and to help him explore church polity and organization and ways unique to Baptists in achieving Christ's objectives for churches.

"Let us look at these content areas in summary . . . The study of Christian theology will help church members deepen their understanding of biblical teachings and organize their beliefs into a personal theology. As a result of these studies, church members should know and express what they believe and apply these beliefs in daily life . . .

"Christian ethics is concerned with God's ideals for living. This has to do with a person's conduct and his obligation for living out the Christlike life in all that he does. It helps a person make the right kind of decisions in the regularity of daily living . . .

"Christian history should be of importance to every church member. From it, he learns about the roots of his faith in Christ, beginning with the revelation of God in Christ. He studies New Testament backgrounds of the church and sees all that God has done in and through the Christian movement. The struggles of churches in the past help him to have perspective concerning problems inherent in his own church . . .

"A study of church polity and organization can help church members to know how and why a Baptist church does its work. This helps the individual to be a more responsible church member, to participate more meaningfully in church activities, and to aid in fulfilling the church's mission." [5]

Skill areas.—The task of training all church members to perform the functions of a church—to worship, witness, educate (learn), minister, and apply—means to develop in members the skill and self-discipline needed to fulfill the mission of a church. Even though the emphasis in this task is on skill development, it assumes a solid foundation of necessary knowledge, understandings, and attitudes on the part of the member. This foundation is built into the lives of members as they regularly participate in study of curriculum areas distinctive to the church's training program and in curriculum areas provided by other church program organizations.

In addition, church members are to be encouraged to reach for even-higher levels of efficiency and effectiveness in performing church functions. The primary focus of training is upon the skills and levels of competence needed by all church members to enable them to function as effective members of the body of Christ in the world.

Church members need to be equipped to function as individuals in all aspects of life and thus fulfill their purpose as members of the body of Christ. In addition, they need to develop skills in participating and working in groups. They need to know how to work in harmonious relationship with one another in small and large groups.

2. Church Member Training Provides Two Approaches

There are two kinds of church member training: ongoing and short-term. Ongoing training is that kind of training that takes place on a regular basis, such as a training group that meets every Sunday evening. Short-term training is the kind of training that has a beginning and an end, such as a one-, two-, three-, or four-session training course.

Opportunities for group study may be offered through regular ongoing training groups or through short-term training to meet special needs or interests of persons. Training in group skills, as well as training in individual skills, will need to be offered at various levels of achievement. Training will also be done on an individual basis with participants being provided self-instruction materials designed to meet individual and distinctive training needs. Because skill development requires practice, training will include activities designed to enable individuals and groups to use the skills being developed.

Sunday evening, prior to the evening worship service, is the best time in most churches to accomplish much of the training that needs to be done. A few churches prefer to schedule training on Sunday morning before or after Bible teaching, or on Sunday evening after the evening service.

Churches may discover that additional training must be scheduled on other days of the week in order to meet all the training needs of the church membership. Some of the groups may meet at the church or at places other than the church building, such as a home or retreat setting. Other groups may meet as breakfast, luncheon, or dinner groups. Many of the activities designed to give members opportunities to practice skills will need to be scheduled at sometime other than Sunday night. Self-instruction may occur anywhere that adequate materials and equipment are available.

The Church Training director, a church member training director, or other leaders selected and elected according to the church's plan are responsible for providing church member training.

VII. What Is Involved in Church Leader Training?

Church leader training may involve training for any leadership role commonly held by church members. To some degree, every believer can be a leader. "Accepting the New Testament concept of the priesthood of believers leads us to include all church members as prospects for leader training. Basic activities of leader training must help all believers to discover and to develop their particular gifts of leadership. No church member can be ignored. He must be given the opportunity to develop. In Christian love we must encourage, guide, and help him to develop the best that is in him." [6]

The task of training church leaders includes training for church-elected places of service, group or class-elected officers (by request of and in cooperation with the particular organization), leaders within short-term projects, or a service rendered informally because of a talent one possesses. All of these training activities fall within the scope of church leader training. The trainee should develop increased competence in order to serve effectively and efficiently. Each leader and member should develop his potential for leadership.

1. Church Leader Training Is Comprehensive

The leader training task includes potential leader training, basic job training, general leadership training, and Christian development courses designed to aid spiritual growth.

Potential leader training is designed to provide fundamental knowledge and understanding and to develop basic skills in the general area of church leadership. It is designed for older youth and adults who are not enlisted for a specific plan of leadership.

Basic job training is training required to enable a person to function in a specific leadership role. It is the training a leader needs to achieve a basic level of performance. Basic job training is the responsibility of each program organization in the church. The Church Training program may assist other organizations as requested.

General leadership training is training that will enable a person to develop as a leader beyond the point of being able to simply function in a given job. General leadership training is for persons already serving in leadership positions. Most general leadership training should be offered by the Church Training program.

Group study and individual study techniques are two approaches frequently used to accomplish this task. In some instances, group and individual approaches may be continued to accomplish a particular training opportunity for a leader or leaders.

Training church leaders can be both preservice and in-service in nature. Preservice training is for persons who have never held a church-elected place of service, who have not recently held a place of service, or who are preparing to accept a different type of leadership responsibility. In-service training is designed to increase the effectiveness of a church member in a leadership role in which he is serving, such as training for an elected Sunday School teacher, Church Training leader, deacon, or church committee member.

Church leader training can be scheduled on Sunday morning or evening and at other times during the week. It can be conducted at the church building or at other places, such as homes or retreat settings.

Church leader training continues to be a top priority concern of church leaders. The continuous need to provide trained leaders is due to rapid turnover of leaders, accelerated growth and expansion of churches, and the many overworked leaders in the churches. This need must be met if churches are to fulfill their mission.

2. Foundational Training Is Provided for Preschoolers and Children

Foundational learning experiences meet the needs of children at a given stage of their development. Appropriate foundations also enable a child, when he becomes competent to do so, to make a personal decision for Christ and church membership. Such training also should make children better able to participate meaningfully in family worship and ministry as appropriate for their stage of development.

3. Skill Training Is Provided for Youth

In addition to the ongoing training activities for youth, several skills activities are provided as a part of the Church Training program. The Youth Bible Drill, Youth Speakers' Tournament, and Youth Week are three youth skills activities that are promoted by the Church Training organization.

The Youth Bible Drill is for younger youth in grades 7–9. It includes four types of drills designed to develop skills in understanding and using the Bible. The Youth Speakers' Tournament is for older youth in grades 10–12. It is intended to appeal to the creative spark within youth for expression of their views and opinions. As much as possible the tournament relates to the Bible as an approach by which youth may develop Bible skills related to interpretation, expression, and study. Church, association, and state eliminations are conducted. State representatives participate in a Bible Drill and Speakers' Tournament demonstration each year at Glorieta and Ridgecrest Baptist Conference Centers.

Youth Week is a laboratory project for the training of youth in church membership. It is a way for Southern Baptist churches to give special recognition to youth as leaders. A youth day or youth month may be promoted instead of a youth week.

Summary

The Church Training program finds expression in a distinctive church program organization. It has been assigned specific tasks to accomplish for the church. This organization is charged with the responsibility of orienting new church members, training church members, and training church leaders. The Church Training program provides study in the areas of Christian theology, Christian ethics, Christian history, and church polity and organization. Because of these facts the Church Training program is essential to a church if its members are to fulfill the role of the church in the world.

Current resource materials to help a church accomplish its church training tasks are available from The Sunday School Board of the Southern Baptist Convention, Nashville, Tennessee.

Notes

1. John Hendrix and Lloyd Householder, *The Equipping of Disciples* (Nashville: Broadman Press, 1977), Foreword. Used by permission.

2. Margaret Sharp, *Church Member Training Manual* (Nashville: Convention Press, 1974), pp. 12–16. Used by permission.

3. Earl Waldrup, *New Church Member Orientation Manual* (Nashville: Convention Press, 1973), p. 3. Used by permission.

4. W. L. Howse and W. O. Thomason, *A Church Organized and Functioning* (Nashville: Convention Press, 1963), pp. 69–70. Used by permission.

5. Philip B. Harris and Lloyd T. Householder, compilers, *Developing Your Church Training Program* (Nashville: Convention Press, 1977), pp. 19–20. Used by permission.

6. Jimmy P. Crowe, *Church Leader Training Handbook* (Nashville: Convention Press, 1974), p. 7. Used by permission.

3.
The Missions Program

The very words *missions* and *missionaries* produce a sparkle in the eyes and hearts of concerned Christians. Perhaps this response always has been true to some degree, but recent years have seen a growing interest in missions among Southern Baptists. An organized concern for missions is a relatively new development in Christian circles, but it seems to be a growing phenomenon of our day.

The Southern Baptist Convention is essentially a testimonial to a concern for missions. The Convention's first impetus was generated by an effort to organize support for world missions. About a century ago an increasing, and at times highly exciting, missionary activity began to characterize Southern Baptist churches. This activity culminated in organizations in the churches for the strengthening of missions. Throughout the United States and in almost ninety countries, missionaries from Southern Baptist churches are serving as ambassadors for Christ. This cooperative enterprise is of great magnitude and is one that grows year by year. God's blessings seem to be upon Southern Baptists as they respond to the Great Commission. These blessings prompted the goal of Southern Baptists to double their total mission force, at home and in other countries, by the end of this century.

One of the many by-products of this missionary zeal has been the realization that Baptists need and want an aggressive emphasis on missions education. Because missions education is essentially a church task, the entire missionary enterprise depends upon church members who know what the Bible teaches about missions, what their personal relationship to missions is, and what their denomination is doing about missions.

I. How Did Missions Education Begin?

"The modern missionary movement began near the close of the eighteenth century. William Carey, a Baptist in England, accepted the personal challenge of carrying the gospel to foreign lands. In the United States young people heard of Mr. Carey, and they responded to missions. Ann and Adoniram Judson and Luther Rice were among the youth from America who became missionaries. Expecting to come in contact with William Carey, these young Congregationalists studied the New Testament on their long voyage. They wanted to be prepared to explain their doctrinal positions. However, their study convinced them that they should be Baptists, too.

Thus the first Baptist missionaries did not start out as Baptists. Halfway around the world, these three young people realized that their new Baptist status left them without support. Luther Rice returned to the United States to stir the hearts of Baptists to mission support.

Baptists organized to support missions in 1814. By 1845 Baptists in the South had separated from those in the North. When the Southern Baptist Convention was organized, two mission boards were created—one for work in the homeland and the other for work in other countries.

As a result of missionaries being sent, mission societies, prayer bands, and other kinds of activities developed among church people. Woman's Missionary Union had its origin in this response to the going of missionaries. Mrs. Ann Baker Graves, whose son was a missionary doctor in China, urged Baptist women to organize in their churches to pray and give money for the spreading of the gospel, particularly among the village women in China. It was Mrs. Graves who called the first national meeting of Southern Baptist women in connection with the Southern Baptist Convention meeting in her own church in Baltimore in 1868. Women responded. They returned to their churches and organized.

By 1888 the women were ready to organize Woman's Missionary Union. They stated the purpose clearly: "to stimulate the missionary spirit and the grace of giving among the women and children of the churches, and aid in collecting funds for missionary purposes." From the very beginning they determined to work within the denomination, educating and supporting rather than sending their own missionaries, as some church women had done.

During the last quarter of the nineteenth century, prominent men began to take a more active part in their churches. Spurred on by missions concern and encouraged by such organizations as the Student Volunteer Movement, men of financial means began to recognize their responsibility for missions. When the Laymen's Missionary Movement began in the United States, Southern Baptist men caught the spirit of the movement.

In 1907 Baptist laymen met to consider what to do. The Convention that year set out the purpose of the Baptist laymen's organization: to "stimulate the zeal and activity of our laymen to a more thorough consecration of their time, prayers, and means to the glory of God in worldwide evangelism." In 1926 the name "Baptist Brotherhood of the South" was adopted. In 1952 the organization became an agency of the Southern Baptist Convention, and the title The Brotherhood Commission was assumed.

Woman's Missionary Union developed as a church organization. Age-level organizations were formed for young people, and boys and girls participated. In the midfifties the missions education program for boys was transferred from Woman's Missionary Union to Brotherhood. Today churches find that these two missions organizations have adapted to provide a well-balanced program of missions education, mission action, and mission support to all members of the church. Many activities can be planned jointly, and the two organizations work together to provide leadership for projects involving men and women, boys and girls in missions.

II. What Do the Missions Programs Do for the Church?

Baptists take great pride in referring to themselves as "missionary Baptists." The tremendous growth in the mission boards and the number of missionaries under appointment creates a vast missions curriculum. Mission expansion demands increased financial support. Hurting, lost humanity in the reach of the church call for mission action. A church needs to organize its concern. Woman's Missionary Union and Brotherhood form the missions program through which a church can carry out its missions tasks.

1. The Missions Programs Create World Awareness

A pastor described the missions organizations as the conscience of his church. This description may be an overstatement, but it is close to the truth. "When we know, we care" is a Baptist slogan from the past, but it speaks to the purpose of missions education.

In the context of the mission organizations, missions designates the work done by a church to fulfill its mission to persons not enrolled or likely to be enrolled in the church or its programs. A church carries out this mission in one of two ways—direct missions and representative missions. Direct missions is a church's direct and personal involvement in ministering and witnessing to people through mission action and establishing church-type missions nearby. Representative missions is what a church does in cooperation with other churches through the association, state convention, and Southern Baptist Convention. Direct missions is *doing*. Representative missions is *supporting* the work that is done by others.

If a church is to be involved in missions directly and through representatives, its members must know what needs exist. They must have an attitude of concern and responsibility for those needs. WMU and Brotherhood seek to create awareness that motivates to action.

2. The Missions Programs Provide Organization for Meeting Need

It is not enough to know about needs; nor is it enough to be concerned. For example, mission study about Japan adds to knowledge. Applied, that study should increase concern for similar situations near at hand. The missions programs provide ways for people to give expression to their concern.

Through organizational mission action and direct evangelism, members are led to participate in missions. Training is provided. Plans are made. Needs are met. The church carries out its missions tasks.

3. The Missions Programs Provide Support for Missions

The individual's part in missions cannot be carried out completely in the local community. The field is the world, and Jesus made his followers responsible for all people in all places.

The missions programs lead persons to support missions by praying, giving money, and providing missionaries. Christians are encouraged to pray for missionaries by name, using birthdays as a means of praying for every missionary at least once during the year. As mission study and missionary speakers help the church member to know more missionaries, then prayer becomes more personal.

WMU and Brotherhood lead the church members in understanding the Cooperative Program and the way that it provides the necessary funding for missions. Woman's Missionary Union leads in special offerings for foreign, home, and state missions.

The missions programs seek to create an environment in the church through which people will hear and respond to God's call to mission service. By keeping members informed about special short-term mission opportunities, WMU and Brotherhood encourage volunteers for projects as well as for missionary careers.

4. The Missions Programs Build a Missions-minded Church

When church members become involved in missions, the interest is contagious. Volunteers respond. Church membership increases as people witness and lead persons to become Christians. Mission study creates a thirst for more information about what God is doing in his world. Reaching goals for the Lottie Moon Christmas Offering brings excitement and satisfaction. The church recognizes itself as a mission-minded church, carrying out the Great Commission in its community and to the ends of the earth.

III. WHAT ARE THE MISSIONS PROGRAMS?

In organizing to function, a church assigns its missions tasks to Woman's Missionary Union and Brotherhood. The work of these two organizations does not overlap any other program in the church. Therefore, if a church does not have these organizations, the missions tasks are not likely to be carried out. Even the smallest church will find that it can function more effectively by having the missions programs.

The simplest kind of missions organization begins with the election of a WMU director and a Brotherhood director. These church-elected officers can work with the pastor in a very small church to provide missions opportunities for the church members. In larger churches, with multiple staff, these two officers can work with the appropriate staff person in completing organization, training leaders, and establishing meeting times.

After age-level organizations are begun and functioning, the WMU director and Brotherhood director continue to work with the church council and appropriate staff in assuring them that missions is a vital part of the total church program.

1. Woman's Missionary Union

Woman's Missionary Union is the organization in a church that provides missions education for women, young women, girls, and preschool boys and girls. WMU is the name of the general organization. Age-level organizations have their own names. Baptist Women is for women over thirty years of age. Baptist Young Women is for women eighteen through twenty-nine years of age. These two adult organizations have monthly meetings for the study of missions. They can also have group meetings, and women join the group that interests them. Mission action groups, prayer groups, and mission study groups are designed to provide specialized participation in missions.

Acteens is the organization for high-school girls, grades 7 through 12. Girls in Action is for girls in grades 1 through 6, and Mission Friends is the preschool organization that includes boys and girls.

Woman's Missionary Union is organized around the tasks that have been assigned to it. These tasks are: teach missions, engage in mission action and direct evangelism, support missions, and provide and interpret information regarding the work of the church and denomination.

There are many good things that a women's organization in a church may do. WMU sees itself as a missionary organization with the responsibility of mobilizing in missions the feminine element of a church.

Woman's Missionary Union seeks to carry out its tasks through organizational meetings; through group meetings for Baptist Women and Baptist Young Women; through leading families and individuals to study missions, support missions, and engage in missions; and through providing leadership for churchwide mission projects.

2. Brotherhood

Brotherhood is the organization a church maintains in order that men and boys can have a consistent program of missions education. It shares responsibility with Woman's Missionary Union for providing opportunities for church members not on the rolls of the missions programs to participate in missions activities.

Brotherhood is the name of the general organization. Baptist Men is the organization for adults, ages eighteen and older. Royal Ambassadors are the boys in the Brotherhood organization; Pioneers are boys in grades 7 through 12, and Crusaders are boys in the first six grades.

The work of Brotherhood is organized around five tasks: engage in missions activities, teach missions, pray for and give to missions, develop personal ministry, and undergird church and denomination.

3. WMU-Brotherhood Joint Actions

There are many things that men and women, boys and girls can do effectively in separate organizations. There are also ways that they can be involved together. Brotherhood and Woman's Missionary Union, the missions programs, work together to give missions leadership in a church.

Joint mission action groups.—Mission action is defined as *the organized effort of a church to minister and witness to persons of special need or circumstance who are not members of the church or its programs.* Some mission action is carried out through short-term projects assigned to youth or adult organizations. Mission action groups are formed to meet needs that cannot be met on a short-term basis. Adult mission action groups are a part of Baptist Men, Baptist Women, and Baptist Young Women organizations.

Mission action groups can also be formed with men and women as members. When the decision is made to form a mission action group thusly, the Brotherhood and WMU directors decide which organization will take the initiative for forming the group. The organization which has the initiative will proceed to set up the group. If Brotherhood leads, then the group leader will be a man, with a woman as the assistant leader. The reverse is true if WMU leads.

Other joint activities.—Baptist Men and Baptist Women may plan joint prayer retreats or mission study classes. Acteens and Pioneers may plan a joint mission action project. Missions Night Out is a plan through which WMU and Brotherhood seek to involve in mission study activities church members who are not members of the missions organizations.

Woman's Missionary Union and Brotherhood are distinct, separate organizations. Their membership is different, and each carries out its own kind of organization and makes its own approach to carrying out its tasks. However, the two organizations are mutually supportive as they seek together to enlist the total church membership in missions activities. Some churches find that scheduling meetings at the same time makes it possible for all members of the family to be in the appropriate missions organization.

Joint churchwide projects.—WMU and Brotherhood may jointly conduct churchwide missions projects. The coordination of WMU-Brotherhood joint action is illustrated in the diagram shown in this chapter.

IV. How Do the Religious Education Ministry and the Missions Programs Relate?

A church can have a missions program of sorts without having WMU and Brotherhood. The pastor may preach an occasional missions sermon or invite a missionary to speak at the church. The church staff may have an annual mission study class; give emphasis to the Lottie Moon Christmas Offering for foreign missions, the Annie Armstrong Easter Offering for home missions; or observe the season of prayer for state missions. A mission bulletin board or a mission film may provide a missions feature.

The minister of education or any other staff minister, however, can strengthen the missions program of a church by establishing WMU and Brotherhood organizations. These two programs have distinctive work to do in a church. That work relates to missions in curriculum and activity.

1. Begin Organizations

To begin organizations, the minister can lead the church to elect a WMU director and a Brotherhood director. He can train these two key officers by using the organization manual for each. The three can study the potential membership and determine which age-level organizations are needed to reach all the church. They can see that leaders for age-level organizations are enlisted and trained. Manuals for leaders of each organization are available in Baptist Book Stores.

To begin the missions organizations in his church, one minister of education recently invited key church leaders from Children's,

Youth, and Adult departments to join him for supper at the church. He explained to them the difference that these organizations could make in the life and work of the church and asked their help in beginning them. The result was that each age-level organization in Brotherhood and Woman's Missionary Union was begun in that church.

Many churches already have well-organized Adult groups. These adults have not felt the challenge to provide missions experiences for youth, children, and preschoolers. In other churches Girls in Action and Crusaders are growing, but there are no organizations for adults, youth, and preschoolers. The missions programs are not complete until every age level in the church has an organization geared to meet its missions developmental needs.

2. Strengthen Existing Organizations

Weak missions programs will result in weak involvement, or no involvement, in missions. Church staff should see that missions materials are included in the church budget. Meetings should be scheduled on the church calendar, and conflicts should be resolved through whatever procedure the church uses in such matters. Ministers of youth and ministers of children and preschoolers need to see the missions organizations as a vital part of the total ministry to the age group. Staff assistance and guidance can be given to leaders of missions organizations and should be a part of the ministry of religious education.

3. Use the Missions Programs in Churchwide Leadership

Church members should be involved in missions. Direct missions is often neglected in the routine activity of church families and individuals. The church often is the last to speak against evils in the community, the last to respond to individual human needs. WMU and Brotherhood should lead the church in missions.

A mission action survey is an important beginning for direct missions. The survey enables the church to discover the needs in the community. Always there will be more needs than one church can meet, so the church decides which needs will be met and by whom. Then the church moves out into the world on mission.

One church recently completed a mission action survey. On the recommendation of the WMU and Brotherhood councils, the church members decided to meet needs in three areas: (1) to minister and witness to an economically deprived area of the city; (2) to help in a juvenile detention home; and (3) to begin a ministry to internationals who lived in the vicinity. Brotherhood took the responsibility for the boys in the detention home, with WMU assuming responsibility for the girls.

A joint mission action group was formed with Baptist Men, Baptist Women, and some men and women who were not members of these organizations previously, to begin English conversation classes with the internationals. Assignments were made to Acteens and Pioneers related to the deprived area, and they began a Big A Club to reach the boys and girls with no church background. Baptist Young Women assumed a leadership role with the Acteens and Pioneers in discovering other ways that needs could be met in that area.

Interestingly enough, from this church two students became summer missionaries with the Home Mission Board. One of the Acteens has surrendered her life to missions, and one of the adult couples in the international class is considering foreign missions as a career.

Mission support projects should include the entire church as often as possible. Woman's Missionary Union began the special mission offerings years ago, but more recently they have become churchwide. The special offerings give church members a way of direct financial support beyond their regular gifts to missions through the Cooperative Program. Other churchwide mission support projects include prayer retreats and activities that help to create an awareness of missions as a career or a short-term way to be involved in missions service.

The study of missions must not be confined to members of WMU and Brotherhood organizations. During the first quarter of each year the study of foreign missions is listed on the denominational calendar. In February the calendar carries dates for the study of home missions. Books are provided for each age level, with undated mission units which can be used for preschoolers. World Missions Conferences planned by associations, weekend missions seminars, and mission field trips are ways that the entire church can become involved in missions education.

4. Guide Enlistment and Enlargement

Enlistment in WMU and Brotherhood refers to reaching persons for membership in organizations. Every member of the church and its programs is a potential member of the missions programs. Efforts should be made regularly to interpret the purpose of WMU and Brotherhood to new members of the church, as well as to members who do not belong.

Enlargement relates to organizations. There should be sufficient organizations, with sufficient leaders, to reach all potential members. Leaders in Brotherhood and WMU should be elected by the church. Church staff should see that they are trained along with other church leaders.

V. WHAT IS THE CHALLENGE OF THE MISSIONS PROGRAMS?

"Let every person in the world have the opportunity to hear and respond to the gospel" is the challenging goal of Southern Baptist missions for the remaining years in the twentieth century. If this goal is to be attained, it will require the total involvement of every Baptist. The missions programs of the church are designed to achieve this involvement and to prepare people for accepting the demands of a lost world.

Traditionally, Woman's Missionary Union has been the prestigious missions organization. In changing roles for women in recent years, as women have joined the labor force, it has been increasingly difficult to adjust meeting times and leadership responsibilities to meet the needs of today's woman. Flexibility in scheduling, simplicity in organization, and contemporary methods for missions education have been the major emphases in WMU planning in recent years. Fewer officers are needed to carry on the work of WMU. Groups provide a variety of missions experiences for women and young women, rather than the traditional missionary program. Flexibility in activity and organization allows a church to decide for itself what kind of WMU program will best suit its needs.

Young adult women are finding that Baptist Young Women, the fastest-growing WMU organization, is tailored to appeal to younger women. With Mission Friends provided for their preschoolers, young mothers can channel their missions interest and zeal into meaningful activities in their church.

Brotherhood has assumed leadership in new areas in recent years. Both in lay renewal and in volunteers for missions projects in crisis situations, Brotherhood is leading men and boys to be participants in missions. New materials are appealing to men, and the growth of Pioneers and Crusaders indicates that the future is bright for Brotherhood.

Perhaps the greatest challenge to the missions programs is to communicate their purpose and program to all the church. Support from church staff is essential if church members are to become participants in missions.

VI. What Resources Are Available?

Curriculum materials are found in magazines for each age-level organization. Brotherhood magazines can be ordered from The Brotherhood Commission, and WMU magazines can be ordered from Woman's Missionary Union. Free interpretive materials can be secured from state WMU and Brotherhood offices. Manuals and other organizational supplies are available through Baptist Book Stores.

COORDINATION OF WMU-BROTHERHOOD JOINT ACTION

Essential Actions	WMU/Brotherhood Age-level Organizations	WMU/Brotherhood Councils or WMU and Brotherhood Directors as Representatives of Councils	Church Council
1. Suggest church-wide projects (on an annual basis)	Suggest projects for year →	Suggest projects and assignment of overall initiative for each project during the year. →	Approve projects to be conducted and assignment of initiative for each project. Add additional projects and make other suggestions if desired
2. Approve projects and assignment of overall initiative for each			
3. Suggest work to be done in conducting a project and the assignment of responsibility (to be completed nearer time when project is to be conducted)		Suggest work to be done and assignment of responsibility to WMU and/or Brotherhood	
4. Approve work to be done and assignment of responsibility			Approve work to be done and assignment of responsibility
5. Make work assignments		Assign work to be done to officers, council, and age-level organizations	(Some assignments may be made to church council members such as Sunday School director, Church Training director)
6. Make detailed plans (with review as necessary)	Make detailed plans for work as assigned	Make detailed plans for work as assigned	
7. Conduct activity	Conduct activity	Conduct activity	
8. Evaluate work	Evaluate work completed by age-level organization	Evaluate work completed by the organization	Evaluate total project

4.
The Church Music Program

A church's music program is a complex and unique design of many experiences and activities. It includes the music experiences of congregational services, church music performance groups, music activity groups, and music study groups. In all these the church family involves itself in music events appropriate to the needs of individuals of all ages to help accomplish the mission of the church.

The music educational experiences are intended to develop musical skills, attitudes, and understandings of persons. These experiences evolve in many ways and are related to the total educational thrust of the church. But the Church Music program is more than educational experience.

I. Music Is a Vital Part of Church Life

The music experiences of the congregational services are a vital part of the church's life. Great congregational singing can be an exciting experience for the church family. The vibrant singing of the gathered congregation joining in songs of praise and testimony can do much to enhance the spirit of the church.

To the church in Corinth Paul the apostle wrote, "I will sing with the spirit, I will sing with the understanding also" (1 Cor. 14:15). Here Paul was saying that the singing should be Spirit-filled and that it should be understood by the singer. Singing is a spiritual experience, and it is an experience that is perceived in the mind—it is to be understood. If there is no understanding, the singing has no meaning. Christian song is the overflow of the

Christian heart. If the heart is full, the singing will likewise be full. Louis F. Benson refers to Christian song as "a spiritual gift which each Christian brings to the sanctuary and contributes to a common song of spiritual fellowship." [1]

To the church at Colosse Paul wrote, "Let the word of Christ dwell in you richly in all wisdom; teaching and admonishing one another in psalms and hymns and spiritual songs, singing with grace in your hearts to the Lord. And whatsoever ye do in word or deed, do all in the name of the Lord Jesus, giving thanks to God and the Father by him" (Col. 3:16–17). There is the direction, the dimension, the declaration, and the desirability of church music.

With reference to this exhortation, Benson explains, "Paul seems to see each singer apart, 'teaching and admonishing one another.' This is because Christian song is to him a purely spiritual function, the natural expression of a heart filled with the Spirit. In his concern that song should flourish among the Colossians he did not exhort them to form music classes but to deepen the spiritual life." [2]

II. MUSIC REQUIRES STRONG LEADERSHIP

The church family looks to the music director for strong leadership, whether he is a full-time staff person, a part-time staff person, or one who gives leadership voluntarily. Whether the person is called a minister of music, a music director, or a congregational song leader, he has opportunities for expressing judgment regarding the music experiences made, shared, or listened to by the congregation. He must choose carefully the hymns and choir music, and he cannot afford the luxury of satisfying his own musical tastes. His judgment in administrative leadership must reflect the broad spectrum of tastes of the congregation as he ministers to their needs in Christian living through the music.

The Church Musician, a monthly music magazine, and *The Cassette Musician,* a quarterly "magazine on tape," provide helpful information for the music director regarding program, administration, and promotion.

III. MUSIC DESERVES SKILLED INSTRUMENTALISTS

While instrumental groups may be used frequently or infrequently, the major responsibility for providing instrumental music—preludes, offertories, postludes—and supportive accompaniment for congregational hymn singing and choral music by the choirs is borne by the organist and the pianist. Skillful playing of these keyboard instruments by persons who sensitively understand the appropriate roles of the organ and piano within the church service can add much to the spirit of the services.

IV. MUSIC CENTERS IN CONGREGATIONAL SINGING

When the church body gathers together, the hymn singing is done by the congregation—all the people together. This unsegregated, ungraded, unorganized body of people, all ages together, made up of some eager singers, some reluctant singers, and some nonsingers, is a group that is involved in "making the music" of hymn singing. Singing together is only one of several possible experiences within the framework of the congregational service that the people do for themselves. If the hymn singing is great and impressive, it is because the people make it so. The music leader cannot produce great singing by himself. The choir cannot make up for a lack of participation by the congregation. At the time of congregational singing, the choir becomes a part of the congregation rather than a group set apart from the remainder of the people.

V. MUSIC IS ENHANCED BY SPECIAL GROUPS

Within the congregational services there are opportunities for individuals to participate in music groups—instrumental and choral—to provide musical experiences in which the remainder of the people are listeners. These groups are usually organized on an age basis—preschool, children, youth, adult. These opportunities not only involve participation in music performance but also focus upon the music development of the individual. In this discussion the use of the word *performance* is intended to mean "the doing of it" rather than "a show, a concert, or a presentation." Unquestioned musical standards—singing or playing in tune, with careful balance and blend, with careful attention to diction of the singers, with awareness of the musical phrase, dynamic levels, and interpretive meaning—are not to be compromised in the church.

The performances of these groups within the congregational service may serve a priestly or a prophetic function. In the priestly role, the choir expresses praise, petition, confession, and so forth to God on behalf of the congregation. The choir sings music that the congregation cannot sing for itself. Here is another dimension of expression much the same as one person voicing a prayer in the service, "leading the prayer," or praying on behalf of all the persons present in the service. This is the priestly role of the choir singing a text addressed to God.

In the prophetic role, the choir may exhort, teach, instruct, warn, or otherwise prophesy to the congregation on behalf of God—singing God's message through scriptural texts or doctrinal truths poetically expressed. In this role the choir speaks to the congregation through the song in the same manner that the preacher speaks to the congregation on behalf of the Lord—the preaching of God's message to God's people.

Usually the major responsibility for the music of the congregational service is given to the adult and youth groups. The frequency of service performance has a high potential with these two age groups. This responsibility for weekly performance places a great significance on the weekly rehearsal schedules. Because of the spiritual, aesthetic, and emotional—as well as musical—values involved, rehearsals bring a warmth and togetherness to a choir that does not always exist in other groups, classes, and so forth, in the church structure. The immediate motivation of the need to make the best possible preparation for a team effort in the congregational services on the next Lord's Day is a matter of keen awareness to all those in the choir.

In these instrumental and choral groups, performance (the doing of it) is a high priority—not for show of virtuosic skills on the part of the choir or director—but because of the need to sing together for the glory of God the right words (the same vowel sounds and consonant execution), the right notes (voices in each part tuned and blended together), and the right rhythm (the rhythm notation executed correctly). Sloppy, mediocre, careless singing is an abomination unto the Lord and is to be studiously avoided in God's house.

At the same time, the musical and vocal development of the individual goes on with the hope that across weeks and weeks of regular rehearsal attendance, the individual will show improvement as a singer, as a music reader, as a member of the team.

VI. Music for Preschoolers and Children Is Largely Educational

The music experiences which the church provides for preschoolers and children (grades 1 to 6) are largely educational in purpose. The children's groups will have some opportunities to make a musical contribution to the congregational services—especially the older children (grades 4, 5, and 6). The preschoolers will be involved in congregational services quite infrequently.

Music is a vibrant, vital source of experience through which preschoolers learn about God, Jesus, the natural world, themselves, and others. All preschoolers enjoy music in some form each time they come to their church, but only fours and fives take part in an organized program of musical experiences.

In considering the values of music in childhood development, it is helpful to understand that songs about God, Jesus, Bible, church, family, self, others, and the natural world help preschoolers form concepts related to Bible truths. Music helps preschoolers experience wonder and joy in a wonderful way. Preschoolers may experience feelings of well-being and personal worth as they sing and are accepted by others. Preschoolers become sensitive to the beauty of music. Music provides opportunities for relaxation and rhythmic response. Music is a medium through which preschoolers find outlets for emotions. Preschoolers may be creative as they make their own tunes, words, or rhythms.[3]

Leadership material for preschoolers is provided in *The Music Leader* with the curriculum units for weekly rehearsals. *Music Times*[4] is a weekly "take home" paper for the preschool child.

VII. MUSIC FOR CHILDREN AIDS CONCEPT DEVELOPMENT

As a child develops and grows through the first six grades of elementary education, music provided in the life of the church takes on increasing significance. For the child music is a source of enjoyment, with an opportunity to participate in activities that let the child sing, move, listen, or create, as he wishes. Music helps bring about the expression of self as music activities—singing, playing instruments, moving, listening—let each child find his or her own expression. Music brings enrichment to the daily routine as natural musical responses can be channeled toward meaningful results. Musical experiences aid concept development—spiritual concepts, musical concepts, and other concepts about self, the world, science, health, family, and friends—as these emerge in the mind and understanding of the child. Music enriches the social and emotional lives of children in this significant area of their growth.[5]

In grouping the children it is usually better to have grades 1, 2, and 3 in one group, and grades 4, 5, and 6 in another group. Leadership material for older children is provided in the quarterly magazine *The Music Leader,* as the curriculum is developed in units of study for the weekly rehearsals. *Young Musicians* is a quarterly magazine designed for these older children.

Leadership material for younger children (grades 1, 2, and 3) is also in *The Music Leader;* and for the younger child there is *Music Makers,* a delightfully colorful magazine published quarterly.

VIII. MUSIC FOR YOUTH BUILDS INVOLVEMENT AND MORALE

Youth is a wonderful age—a time of discovery, of learning, of experimentation. Musical growth has heightened the abilities to understand and grasp. Physical development has brought a maturity to the singing voice, and the boy sopranos and altos have become sturdy tenors and basses. The thrill of sharing in ensemble singing—in voice parts, two, three, four, or more—brings musical excitement unknown in earlier ages. Greater frequency of performance is now possible. Choir retreats and choir tours are new areas of keen interest involving musical, social, and witnessing and mission endeavors that build strong morale. The accomplishment of excellent performance brings a sense of inner warmth truly felt only by those who have paid the price in rehearsal, determination, and discipline.

Opus One is a quarterly music magazine designed for younger youth (sometimes referred to as junior high age). Some of the boys' voices have changed; some are still changing; and some have just begun to change. The voice ranges of these groups with specific problems need special attention to maintain high interest and full participation in the choir.

Opus Two is a quarterly music magazine designed for older youth (sometimes referred to as senior high age). Here is general music for two, three, or four parts—soprano, alto, tenor, bass—as these young people stand on the threshold of vocal adulthood and discover the joy of a maturing singing voice.

IX. MUSIC FOR ADULTS IS RICHLY REWARDING

From eighteen to eighty and past is a joyful lifetime of abundant experiences in music in the life of the church. In so many ways can an adult find satisfying involvement and expression in music activity—singing, playing, sharing, listening, helping others to enjoy great sounds of music. How blessed is the adult whose church makes possible a wide variety of musical opportunities both in kind and caliber, both in variety of literature and variety of sounds, and with leadership of tall stature giving intelligent direction. Presently, unique opportunities for church music involvement exist in work with single and senior adults.

Gospel Choir and *Choral Praise* are music magazines for adult choirs and are published quarterly. *Gospel Choir* contains choral music with some evangelical message and sound in the broad stream of gospel tradition. *Choral Praise* presents exciting sounds of choral music somewhat more traditional and classic in content and style. Both music magazines are fresh, contemporary, and immediately singable by adult choirs.

X. CURRICULUM MATERIALS FOR YOUTH AND ADULTS ARE READILY AVAILABLE

Study materials for youth and adult in the Church Music program may be found in the Church Study Course. Here is a wide choice of materials that may be used in short-term educational ventures, either in group experience or in individual study. Personal development in the pursuit of these studies improves skills in singing, playing, and reading musical notation. Attitudes and understandings are sharpened and made more meaningful as knowledge of church music history, the development of Christian hymnody, and the broad sweep of the historic heritage of church music literature become part of a person's Christian experience.

In addition to the materials already mentioned, there is a wealth of material for persons who are music leaders or who desire to serve in a leadership capacity with any age group. Unfolding understandings of methodology and teaching techniques increase the capacity for leadership in the church's music program, and these are provided for in the church music portion of the Church Study Course.

XI. MUSIC UNDERGIRDS ALL RELIGIOUS EDUCATION PROGRAMS

In the other structures of our church life—Sunday School, Church Training, Woman's Missionary Union, and Brotherhood—the sounds of music are woven tightly into the warp and woof of their activities. Songs appropriate to each age level are usually part of the total experience at each meeting. Songs and hymns help reaffirm biblical truths and doctrinal beliefs. Songs and hymns appropriate to the dated curriculum help to reinforce the truths inherent in the lesson material. The Scriptural Index of Hymns and the Index of Scriptural Bases for the Hymns, as well as the Topical Index, will help to make the *Baptist Hymnal* a curriculum companion for these programs.

Excellent opportunities are afforded for the use of musical talent in department activities. Song leaders and pianists, as well as individuals, ensembles, and groups providing special music, can provide music leadership in these departments. Playing the piano in Sunday School or Church Training can afford excellent training opportunities for young pianists. Young people with potential keyboard ability should be sought out and utilized in this way.

The hymn singing of these departments can effectively be related to the hymn singing of the congregational services. In department opportunities new hymns can be learned to heighten the participation in the congregational services. The department music leader is actually leading a segment of the congregation, and he can bring helpful emphasis to increase the participation in the church services.

XII. Summary

God in his Word exhorts us to praise him, to "Come before his presence with singing" (Ps. 100:2). In his church, in all its activities, music is a vital experience. It voices praise; it testifies to the power of the gospel for salvation; it bears witness to the vitality of the Christian life. Music reaches the unreached; it penetrates behind closed doors; it communicates Christian love and understanding; it calms and heals and brings comfort. Those persons who have leadership responsibility in all areas of church life should wisely seek ways to use the musical resources within the congregation in the most effective ways.

I. E. Reynolds has succinctly stated the challenge of music: "If the Bible makes so much of music, you cannot afford to touch it lightly. If music has such universal appeal, it means you have an approach to every heart. If it is the stay of a burdened heart, you are a messenger of rest to all that are weary. If it inspires and teaches, you are an uplifter and teacher for all to whom your music may speak. It is yours to keep it from any low standard, and to direct and use it for the uplifting of men and the glory of God." [6]

Notes

1. Louis F. Benson, *The Hymnody of the Christian Church* (Richmond: John Knox Press, 1956), p. 44.

2. Ibid.

3. Florence Conner Hearn, *Guiding Preschoolers* (Nashville: Convention Press, 1969), pp. 67–71.

4. The first issue of *Music Time* will begin with the January 1979 issue.

5. Bill F. Leach, Saxe Adams, Talmadge Butler, and Terry Kirkland, compilers, *Music for Today's Children* (Nashville: Broadman Press, 1975), p. 5.

6. I. E. Reynolds, *A Manual of Practical Church Music* (Nashville: Sunday School Board of the Southern Baptist Convention, 1923), p. 25.

Part III
The Vocational Roles in Religious Education

1. The Role of the Pastor in Religious Education
John T. Sisemore, Director of the Sunday School Division, Baptist General Convention of Texas, Dallas, Texas

2. The Minister of Education
Harry M. Piland, director, Sunday School Department, Baptist Sunday School Board, Nashville, Tennessee

3. The Minister of Education and Music
J. Kenneth Robinson, Minister of Music and Education, Meadows Baptist Church, Plano, Texas

4. The Minister of Adult Education
Alva G. Parks, Associate Professor of Education Administration, Southwestern Baptist Theological Seminary, Fort Worth, Texas

5. The Minister of Youth Education
Philip H. Briggs, Professor of Youth Education, Southwestern Baptist Theological Seminary, Fort Worth, Texas

6. The Minister of Childhood Education
Jimmye Winter, Girls in Action—Mission Friends Consultant, Woman's Missionary Union, Birmingham, Alabama

7. The Minister of Preschool Education
Gail Linam, Director of Preschool Education, Calvary Baptist Church, Waco, Texas

1.
The Role of the Pastor in Religious Education

Would most pastors agree that their church is limited primarily by the quality of the educational program? Would you agree that a pastor ought to think of religious education as the most significant part of the life and work of the church? Would it be logical to assume that a pastor should give more time and attention to the educational aspects of the church than to any other?

Many pastors and even some church members would consider these questions and their implications as unrealistic, if not unacceptable. But are they? Is it not true that the cause of most church inadequacies is the failure of the members to *know, be,* and *do* what they should as Christians? Do not these failures arise from an inadequate or improper religious education background on the part of the people?

Think for a moment of the incalculable consequences of education. Knowledge is the outcome of education. Attitudes yield to education. Goals are reappraised through education. Values change because of education. Life-styles evolve as a result of education. Personality is improved by education. Character is formed by education. Achievement is advanced through education. And by simply adding the word *Christian* in front of all those nouns, the far-reaching significance of religious education becomes immeasurably important to the Christian, the church, and the pastor.

If the foregoing logic is valid, the pastor has a most urgent role in religious education—as desirable or undesirable as it may seem.

Here are some practical suggestions for the pastor who is serious about his total responsibility for the effectiveness of his church.

I. REVIEW THE SCOPE OF GOD'S CALL

The Bible teaches that all believers have a twofold call: the call to redemption in Christ and the call to servantship for Christ. Each person who responds to the call to redemption becomes a member of the priesthood of which Christ is the High Priest (Heb. 4:14). As a member of this royal priesthood the believer is a minister (*diakonos*). These basic truths come to one indisputable conclusion: *All believers are called to be ministers of Jesus Christ.*

God also calls his priests to special forms of service, at special times, in special places, for special purposes. Therefore, the call "to preach" is a blessed reality. However, if the phrase "to preach" is interpreted in the narrow sense as meaning preaching only, then there is a gross misunderstanding of what preaching really involves.

In Paul's letters to Timothy he included the ability to teach as one of the prerequisites for being a pastor: "above reproach, the husband of one wife, temperate, prudent, respectable, hospitable, able to teach" (1 Tim. 3:2, NASB). "And the things which you have heard from me . . . entrust to faithful men, who will be able to teach others also" (2 Tim. 2:2, NASB).

On two occasions Paul testified to the fact that he had been called to be "a preacher, an apostle, and a teacher." (See 1 Tim. 2:7; 2 Tim. 1:11). In Ephesians 4:11 Paul also linked to the work of a minister the dual roles of preaching and teaching. He further demonstrated his belief in the full scope of preaching by remaining at Ephesus for a year and one-half to teach the believers who had responded to his preaching.

When God calls a person into the pastoral ministry, it is a twofold call. The call certainly centers in preaching, but it just as surely includes responsibility for the teaching aspect of the ministry. To fail to assume the educational role along with the proclamation role is to be unresponsive to the full scope of God's call. Furthermore, the neglect or disparagment of education is to guarantee an incomplete if not an ineffective ministry and to shortchange a church in its most basic approach to its God-given task.

II. Assume Responsibility for a Total Ministry

As is generally the case, a strong emphasis on one side of an issue may result in an underemphasis on the other side. For a long time, perhaps ever since the art of preaching became a profession, the companion aspect of the pastoral ministry—education—has often been neglected and sometimes held in disdain. To be sure, there are important differences between preaching and teaching. However, those differences do not justify neglect of one in favor of the other. An appropriate balance between these twin responsibilities is sorely needed if a pastor is to have a total ministry.

1. Recall the Early Emphasis on Education

In the Old Testament, especially in the Torah, the home was identified as the primary institution of learning. This home education program was essentially religious education and came under the responsibilities of the father. In addition to the home, the tribe of Levi had the specific function of being the priests in Israel. The priests were the official teachers of the Jewish people. Gradually the priests became ineffective and sometimes corrupt in their assignment, with the consequences that the people failed to follow them or support what they did.

It is generally thought that the failure of the priests brought the role of the prophet into the foreground. By default the prophets became the official voice of the Law. They studied the Law, copied it, interpreted it, and gradually became the religious educators in Israel.

Following the exile, the rabbi (teacher and scribe) became the leader and final authority in religion and religious education. In Judaism then, and even today, there was no more exalted position than that of the rabbi. To show disrespect or to question his authority was unthinkable. It was equated with discrediting God himself.

2. Remember the Place of Teaching in Christ's Ministry

At least sixty times Jesus was called "Rabbi," and in thirty other instances he was addressed as "Master" (teacher). This title was reserved for those outstanding persons who taught the things of God especially in their reference to man's duty (education!). The pastor who identifies himself and his own ministry with that of Christ needs to remember that Christ was regarded primarily as a teacher. In only 143 passages is he referred to as a preacher (or as preaching), but in 217 he was alluded to as a teacher (or as teaching).

Jesus taught frequently, and the crowds delighted in his teaching. Friend and foe alike were attracted to his teaching so much that the daily routines at the Temple and in the synagogues were disturbed and the Roman government was dismayed. Nicodemus recognized the great effect of Christ's teaching when he said, "Rabbi, we know that you have come from God as a teacher" (John 3:2, NASB).

3. Rethink the Educational Work of the Early Church

The book of Acts is in many ways a record and a report on the educational activities of the apostles and the early leaders of the church. "And they were continually devoting themselves to the apostles' *teaching*" [author's italics] (Acts 2:42, NASB). "And as they were speaking to the people, the priests and the captain of the temple guard, and the Sadducees, came upon them, being greatly disturbed because they were *teaching* [author's italics] the people" (Acts 4:1-2, NASB). "And . . . they kept right on *teaching* [author's italics] and *preaching* [author's italics] Jesus as the Christ" (Acts 5:42, NASB).

The exact nature of the educational organization and methodology of the early churches is not completely clear. However, the content of their teaching is contained in the Gospels. The term *kerygma* is applied to this material. In its simplest form it revealed (1) how Jesus came, (2) what Jesus did, (3) what Jesus taught, (4) why Jesus died, and (5) how Jesus lives. These facts are amplified in other books of the New Testament. False or inaccurate teachings concerning these truths were also addressed by the non-Gospel writers, especially Paul.

After the dispersion of the Christians from Jerusalem, the new converts were primarily Jewish proselytes and Gentiles. The Gentile cultures were pagan and often vile. Persons coming from such backgrounds had many problems which plagued the churches, such as the one at Corinth. These new Christians needed a great deal of teaching and instruction because their growth and development was often slow and erratic. Religious education was not only inherent in Christianity; it was an absolute essential to the survival of the churches.

It is quite possible that Paul's interpretation of the Scriptures in 2 Timothy 3:15-17 is also a significant clue to the kind of instruction that was included in the education efforts of the early churches.

III. Interpret the Significance of Religious Education

If the Great Commission includes education (teaching and training), and it does, then a church needs to be aware of this fact, to understand its meaning, and to know what is involved. Only a pastor can adequately fill the role of interpreter in this important matter.

1. Teach the Biblical Basis of Education

The educational emphasis in the Old Testament was not set aside in the New Testament. Rather, it was greatly enlarged and more fully developed. This expanded emphasis grows out of the very nature of the gospel. It requires an educational approach to its proclamation, interpretation, application, and internalization.

The first chapter of this book is a treatment of the biblical background for church education programs. These concepts may be capsulized as follows: (1) Education has a strong Old Testament base; (2) education is magnified in the New Testament; (3) Jesus called, trained, and sent his disciples to win and teach the lost;

(4) Jesus committed his church to educational work as a major tool in accomplishing its mission; (5) Jesus promised his abiding presence; and (6) pastors today have the unique privilege of guiding churches in their total work through the educational phases of the ministry.

2. Magnify the Educational Objectives of the Church

Most churches do not have a formal statement of their educational objectives. This absence of objectives may account for the fact that many church members have little or no idea why their church exists or what it should be doing.

All education programs must have a firm philosophical base. Baptists rightly insist that the foundation for everything a church does be based on the Holy Scriptures. Thus the philosophy of religious education must be a biblical philosophy. The Bible presents the goal of the Christian life as progress toward spiritual maturity. This goal therefore becomes the overarching objective of a church. Because spiritual growth and maturity are continuous, ongoing, lifelong processes, this objective is always relevant and always challenging.

Although the overarching goal is progress toward Christian maturity, this goal must be more definitive when it is applied to the educational setting. There are seven distinct areas of growth that are involved in the Christian context. These special areas, the base out of which age-level objectives are formulated, were formalized by The Sunday School Board of the Southern Baptist Convention and published in the *Church Program Guidebook*.[1] They are as follows:

Christian conversion.—To lead each person to a genuine experience of the saving grace of God through Jesus Christ.

Church membership.—To guide each Christian into intelligent, active, and devoted membership in a New Testament church.

Christian worship.—To help each person make Christian worship a vital and constant part of his expanding experience.

Christian knowledge and conviction.—To help each person grow toward mature Christian knowledge, understanding, and conviction.

Christian attitudes and appreciations.—To assist each person in developing such Christian attitudes and appreciations that he will have a Christian approach to all of life.

Christian living.—To guide each person in developing habits and skills that promote spiritual growth and in applying Christian standards of conduct in every area of life.

Christian service.—To lead each person to invest his talents and skills in Christian service.

All religious education programs, projects, and activities should grow out of and contribute to these or some similar set of objectives. Such objectives serve as guidelines for programming and as checkpoints in evaluation. Therefore, the pastor needs to keep the church aware of these great goals of God's grace.

3. Develop a Strong Sense of Educational Commitment

The educational attitudes and commitments of a church eventually reflect those of the pastor. A large attendance at worship services and a small attendance at educational experiences are not necessarily a compliment to a pastor's preaching ability. The attendances may be a reflection of the way the congregation believes the pastor feels about education or a response to an educational program that is not challenging. Too often churches fail to fulfill their mission because the pastor appears to regard education as an optional, if not an unimportant, aspect of church work. Such an attitude seems to correlate with a large number of uncommitted, untrained, uninvolved church members. When church members have no sense of direction or progress, the church will fall short of its potential. As a consequence the pastor will fail to reach his greatest usefulness.

These cause-and-effect outcomes are ample reasons for a pastor to develop a strong sense of direction for the educational program and to invest a reasonable amount of time, energy, and influence in finding suitable educational objectives for his church.

4. Work to Develop Converts into Disciples

The Great Commission requires the making of *disciples,* not just converts. Obviously a disciple must first be a convert, but being born again is only the beginning place in discipleship. A disciple is one who not only knows Christ as Savior, but one who is a faithful follower, an adherent, a facsimile, a personification of the one from whom he learned. In the case of a Christian disciple, one must become a reproduction of the Master Teacher in his beliefs, qualities, and character.

Jesus chose only twelve men to become his apostles. Through three and one-half years of diligent education he brought them to a high level of discipleship. They failed miserably at times, even under the tutelage of the greatest teacher; but they eventually became disciples through the long and often painful process of teaching and learning. Through this process of education the apostles became more than converts. They became *disciples.*

Churches today are full of converts who are not disciples primarily because they have not been properly educated. Very often it is the minister alone who can provide the initial impetus for making the educational programs productive enough to develop disciples. Because education is required for making converts into disciples, no other ministerial function is as important to the life and work of a church.

IV. BECOME A QUALIFIED LEADER IN RELIGIOUS EDUCATION

If a church is to be effective in its educational support of the gospel, the pastor must be more than a passive observer of the work. He must do more than give lip service to this phase of his ministry. The most effective pastors at this time in history are the ones who are genuine leaders in the educational program. This observation holds true in all kinds of churches, regardless of size or location.

To be a qualified leader does not mean to be the one and only education worker. The do-it-yourself concept is not a good approach to leadership. A good leader gets his work done through other people, but he is always a qualified person in the field of his leadership.

Unfortunately many pastors seem to have been cheated in their preparation for the ministry. They have had little instruction in how to operate a church program of education. Therefore, the pastor who is concerned about the education work in his church will find it necessary to be largely self-taught. Fortunately there are many opportunities for such learning. Each of the following suggestions is based on the assumption that the pastor has a conviction that education is an integral part of his ministry and a priority concern of the church.

1. Research the Education Disciplines

Reading, surveying, conferring, and investigating are important words. They imply a planned use of time, but they produce very significant values from time so used.

The reading of this entire book would serve as a strong beginning for any pastor. There is no other source for Southern Baptists that includes all of the features of this book. Part 1 presents the biblical, theological, and philosophical foundations on which religious education is based. Part 2 describes and defines the Southern Baptist programs of religious education. Part 3 outlines the various phases of the educational ministry and the duties of the educational specialists and staff members.

In addition to this book, each of the church program organizations (Sunday School, Church Training, Brotherhood, Woman's Missionary Union, and Music) has a basic program book for the general leaders of that particular program. These program organizations also have numerous age-group books which provide ample information for a pastor. All of these books are available from the Baptist Book Stores.

The most current information is found each month in the leadership periodicals produced by the various program organizations. The "how-to" aspects of the program are found in these publications.

For a pastor time is a precious commodity. However, two or three hours in study each week will make it possible for a pastor to be well informed and even to become an expert in a most significant part of his ministry. With a little attention to life-style priorities, almost anyone can find two or three hours per week for self-instruction.

2. Take Advantage of Update Opportunities

Each of the state Baptist organizations has personnel available for conferences, interpretation of materials, and projects to provide help for pastors with their educational work. Cooperative Program funds make these services available—and they are valuable.

Numerous services and materials are also available from the various program offices of the Southern Baptist Convention. There are opportunities galore for keeping up with developments in every aspect of church life. In no way does a pastor subordinate his pastoral work or prophetic ministry by qualifying in his education responsibilities. In fact, the very opposite is true. He will greatly enhance his total ministry and improve his total performance as a minister of Jesus Christ.

3. Use Educational Approaches to Improve Church Life

Many untapped opportunities to improve the whole of church life are available to the pastor who sees education as a uniquely spiritual aspect of his ministry. To be sure, teaching and training are not very glamorous activities. They are slow and even tedious approaches to church advance, but they are productive and lasting ways to get the best things done. Christian maturity is a long-term goal, and character development is difficult to achieve; but both are the fruit and the reward of the patient educator.

Spectacular results are not often achieved by the education process, but the wise pastor knows that this divinely given process assures a quality of outcome not found in any other approach. Above all, results that are educationally induced are lasting. They abide after a pastor has gone to another field; and they remain as a monument to the wisdom, skill, and commitment of a leader who has taken seriously the command to make *disciples*.

V. Use the Program Organization Leaders in Lieu of Staff

Some pastors experience a tension that arises over the fact that they like the preaching aspect of the ministry, but they dislike or feel insecure in the educational functions. Pastors having this problem will need to discipline themselves to discharge their educational responsibilities until they learn to enjoy doing them as well as they enjoy preaching. However, there is also a very bright side to this preaching and educating dichotomy. It does not have to be an either/or matter. It can and should be a both/and matter. Furthermore, a pastor can use to advantage, and with great profit, the church-elected leaders in the education organizations to enrich and support his total ministry. He can use them in lieu of paid staff. If a pastor has staff members, some of this responsibility will be delegated to them; but his accountability remains. When he does use the organizations, every moment of time given to their leadership will be amply rewarded in innumerable ways, even in improved preaching.

1. Lead in the Planning Activities

Every organization will do *something,* even if it is nothing more than using its energy in maintaining itself. How much better to discover the unique contributions the organizations can make and to lead them in achieving their highest potential!

All leadership begins with planning. It really is true that a plan without a man is worthless and that a man without a plan is useless. But a man with a plan is priceless.

In leading the planning process a good place to start is with an annual planning retreat. All of the program leaders (church council) may meet with the pastor to determine three or four basic goals for the new church year. The leaders within each of the programs would follow this general planning with specific plans for the organizations. Obviously the program organization plans would relate to and support the general church goals.

The pastor is the logical person to present, interpret, and lead the church to approve and support the plans. The pastor would also confer with the program leaders to check on progress, secure reports for the church, and evaluate the results of the organizations in carrying out their plans.

The church program organizations have plan books or planning helps available from the appropriate agencies. Each state will have important plans and events that need to be considered. Most associations also provide planning input and material. Every church has knowledgeable members who may provide ample resources to guide and assist in the program planning activities.

In addition to annual planning, the pastor may want to lead the organizations to do long-range planning and probably some short-term planning as well. The key to success in all planning efforts is to plan *with* the appropriate people—never *for* them.

2. Guide the Nominating Committee

Most churches do a reasonably good job of providing a nominating committee for the selection of program leaders. However, it is often true that the committee does not know the requirements of the positions they are to fill. The pastor may render a most valuable service and avoid numerous difficulties if he will meet with the committee, share with them the needs of the positions to be filled, and give them suggestions about procedures. He may also meet with the committee periodically to check on progress and to provide support and assistance. Probably no greater contribution to the work can be made by a pastor than the assistance he gives in getting the right person in the right place at the right time.

3. Develop an Effective Leadership Corps

Helping church workers become more proficient in their work is either the strength or the weakness of a pastor's educational leadership. Weakness at this point shows up in a lack of personnel to fill the positions, poor quality of work, short terms of service, low attendance, numerous dropouts, decline in the number of organizational units of work, and a general sense of frustration and despair. Admittedly, the pastor cannot be faulted for all of these problems; but it is amazing how many of these enigmas are solved when the pastor becomes concerned enough to exercise strong leadership in the training of the volunteer workers of the church.

No one approach to leadership training is best or even adequate to meet the total need for successful workers. A well-planned and comprehensive continuing approach is required. A good Church Training program is an essential part of a good leadership development plan. Regular use of the various study course materials is also vital. A continuing plan for selecting and training potential leaders is highly recommended. Probably a personal conference with the workers to discover needs and design a special study program for each one is the most strategic and fruitful way to develop strong lay leadership.

The foregoing suggestions may well stimulate the typical response: "Our church is small; I'm too busy to do all of that." Right! That is exactly why it needs to be done. The smaller the church, the more critical the need for the pastor's help in leadership development. And there is probably no other way for a pastor to get time for other things until he makes time to secure more workers that are properly equipped. The pastor who takes seriously the challenge of training and developing more workers is facing up to the fact that he is responsible to God "for the equipping of the saints."

4. Provide the Essential Leadership Meetings

Leadership meetings are as important to the success of an organization as practice sessions are to any team-type sport. And no one plays a more important role in having successful church program organization meetings than the pastor. He is the only one who can take the lead in getting calendar time, securing attendance, and making sure that the meetings are accomplishing their purposes.

The typical excuses for not having leadership meetings are well known, and there is little to be gained in refuting them. It should be obvious that meetings that are not needed should not be held. By the same logic, it seems that meetings that *are* needed should be scheduled, well planned, expertly conducted, and concluded as soon as their purpose is served. Only the persons whose job assignments require their attendance should be invited or expected to attend. If the number is small, that is not a problem.

When workers complain about too many meetings, they are simply saying that they have too many responsibilities that require attendance at meetings. These leaders may also be overextended in nonchurch activities that require meetings.

Any given church may not be able to have all of the organizations it needs or wants. But if it fails to provide leadership meetings for all of the organizations it has, there is little hope for any worthwhile accomplishments. Therefore, the pastor's attitude toward meetings is crucial. No one likes to meet every night. However, in church life, meetings are an occupational requirement. But they are rewarded by the joys and blessings of being a leader. It should also be remembered that the most meaningful relationships with the church members are frequently tied to the organizational meetings. Just as Peter, James, and John formed the inner circle of the apostles, the organizational leaders in a church form the inner fellowship of the church. It is in these relationships that the essence of the fellowship is developed and where the pastor's influence is most beautifully rewarded.

5. Work for Continuity in Leadership

Far too many church members look upon election to office as a one-year "sentence" to be served with freedom as the reward at the end of the term. This feeling is a destructive attitudinal problem that desperately needs to be corrected. Therefore, one of the finest contributions a pastor can make to the education program is the stabilization and lengthening of the tenure in all leadership positions.

When a new church year begins, a leadership recognition banquet would be helpful. This banquet could be a time of fellowship, inspiration, motivation, and commitment to the new year's work. It seems nothing short of tragic for a church to go for years without any recognition of the faithful and devoted people who serve on and on in a volunteer capacity.

The pastor should welcome every opportunity to counsel, encourage, and affirm the workers. To be unapproachable and unresponsive to the workers or to overlook the supportive opportunities that arise will be to face the inevitable problem of replacing discouraged and unhappy workers. Furthermore, the time already invested in these workers will be lost; and they will likely end up in the army of ex-workers, the number of which is already overwhelming in many churches.

The pulpit provides the pastor his finest opportunity to create an attitude of willingness, dedication, and continuity of leadership to the educational program of a church. Proclaiming the biblical truths about education; pointing out the significance of the educational activities; teaching the expectations of God in the use of time and talent; building a reliance on the power of the Scriptures, the leadership of the Holy Spirit, and the transforming grace of Christ—these are the ways in which a pastor renders immeasurable service to the church. At the same time he will discover that his own accomplishments are being greatly multiplied as he uses the church organizations to fulfill his own call to be a minister.

But there is more. In the process he will probably become as effective as an educator as he is as a preacher. Then he can fully claim Christ's promise, "I am with you always" (Matt. 28:20, NASB) because he will be making *disciples*.

Note

1. *Church Program Guidebook* (Nashville: Convention Press, 1964), pp. 140–142.

2.
The Minister of Education

Persons who have led in religious education have not always been known as ministers of education. In earlier years, some were called paid superintendents. Later such persons were termed educational directors, associate pastors, or assistants to the pastor. Some were and are called directors of Christian education. Today some are given the title program coordinators; others are called administrators. To define more accurately the widening scope of the position, increasing numbers are called ministers of education and administration. Most of us today, however, are probably known as ministers of education; and that title is well suited to the task. Let it be said, however, that the title is not nearly as important as the man—what he is and what he does.

When we refer to title in this chapter, the term *minister of education* will be used. As reference is made to the person who is a minister of education, the pronoun *he* and the noun *man* will be used frequently. This usage is not intended to indicate any bias toward men in the ministry of education—for since the beginning, some women as well as men have served as ministers of education.

I will attempt to deal with four question areas in this chapter. *First,* who is the minister of education? What is he like, and what are his qualifications? Can they be identified? *Second,* what does he do? Can his basic tasks be identified and described? *Third,* what are his special relationships? He has many relationships, but are some so special that they are keys to his effectiveness? *Fourth,* what can he expect to receive? It is not implied that he serves for rewards, but it is true that he will receive positive benefits and satisfactions that accrue directly from his task.

I. Who He Is

The minister of education is a person called of God to help a church find and reach persons for Bible study, seek to lead them to Christ, and help them grow and develop in his likeness.

1. He Is Called of God

Whatever else he is, the minister of education must be called of God. Nothing else will sustain a minister of education in the times of trial, difficulties, temptations, frustrations, and burdens that will inevitably come if he remains in the work long enough. Every minister of education should be able to say with the apostle Paul, "I am 'an apostle of Christ Jesus by the *will of God* [author's italics]' " (Eph. 1:1, RSV), and "How thankful I am to Christ Jesus our Lord for *choosing me* [author's italics] as one of his messengers" (1 Tim. 1:12, TLB). The clear and positive conviction that "God called me" is a bulwark of strength whatever the conditions or place in which he serves. It is a qualification of the minister of education without which he must not even begin. Not only will the call of God sustain, but there is no other reason to serve as a minister of education. Only a positive, sure call is sufficient.

Of course, calls can and do come in various ways because each person is different. One person may have felt a sense of calling since a young child, while another may have recognized his call later in life. One may have felt the call of God at a definite time and place, another as a settling conviction that seemed to deepen with each passing day. Whatever it is and however it comes, let the call come from God and let it be the clear and positive indicator that leads one to serve as a minister of education.

2. He Is Called to Minister

The word *minister* often refers to a pastor, a spiritual guide, or one who is given charge of an area of service. That is not the sense of the word I have in mind, although the minister of education is frequently an ordained minister. One meaning of the word minister, according to Webster, is "to give aid and service." That definition is on target. The minister of education does give aid and service both to pastor and people. It is not a degrading concept at all to say that the minister of education helps the pastor. He is, in a sense, the pastor's "right arm."

The minister of education also helps and serves the people of the church and the people in the city where he serves. He should never be aloof from or above the people. Always, his place is with the people. He must help and serve the "up and ins" and the "down and outs." He must serve and help both the rich and the poor and the strong and the weak; and he must always minister in Jesus' name. If the minister of education should desire greatness, let him remember that the Scripture says, "Let him who would become great become the servant of all" (Mark 10:43–44, author's paraphrase). Oswald Sanders wrote: "True greatness, true leadership is achieved not by reducing men to one's service but in giving oneself in selfless service to them." [1]

3. He Loves People

The minister of education must love people. He will never succeed without that quality. He must love *many* people, for he will work closely with hundreds. He has close, intimate relationships in all the organizations and groups in the church. Loving a few will not do it. He must love *all* kinds of people, for they come in various races and temperaments. He must love people who are different from him. That is not an easy thing to do.

Ministers of education will never have 100 percent cooperation. People will take different views; therefore, conflict will develop. I will never forget such an incident in my ministry. On the occasion of an important committee meeting at the church, I grew impatient in the course of that meeting and spoke words that should have been left unspoken. Following the meeting, on my way home, I turned my car around, drove to the home of the offended committee member, walked to the house, and rang the doorbell. Forgiveness was asked for and received. There was a time of prayer and reconciliation between me and the fellow member. No member of that church was closer to me in the days to follow.

Truly a genuine love for people can be used of God as can nothing else. Sanders says it in simple but profound fashion: "The spiritual leader is a lover of men." [2] Love is truly the distinguishing mark of discipleship. It was Jesus who said, "A new commandment I give to you, that you love one another" (John 13:34, RSV). That love should not be confined to persons who are members of the church or just to persons easy to love. Jesus said, "Love your enemies and pray for those who persecute you" (Matt. 5:44, RSV).

4. He Has the Ability to Work with People

One may possess a love for people and still fail to relate to them successfully. It is of great importance that a minister of education have the ability to work with people in a successful and effective manner. If one were working with machines or figures, this ability would not matter as much; but a leader of people must learn how to work with people. This principle cannot be overestimated. Les Giblin wrote, "In a study at Carnegie Technological Institute, it was found that ninety percent of all working people who fail in their life's vocation fail because they cannot get along with people." [3]

I have seldom seen a person fail in his task without his inability to work with people being at least a part of the failure. The opposite is also true. One's success is often directly related to his ability to get along with people. Lawrence Appley goes even farther in writing, "Working satisfactorily with people is not part of the management job—it is the entire job." [4]

This ability to relate to people implies learning how to listen, to understand, to motivate, and to teach. It means "seeing something through the eyes of another." Whatever it takes to improve one's ability to relate to people, it must be done. The minister of education will never find fulfillment or effectiveness without it.

5. He Is Willing to Work

Work is required of the minister of education. He will have more than he can do. He must never shrink from work. The longer one stays in a church, the more there is to do, no matter how much he gets done. The secret, of course, lies in the principle of sharing the work load. Sometimes he must say a simple no; but the fact remains—no lazy ones should assume that the job of minister of education is for them. They will quickly discover their error.

Let it also be said that a minister of education will never really come to the end of a day or a week or a year and be able to say, "I've done all there was to do; my work is finished." There's always more. Dr. James Harris, pastor of University Baptist Church in Fort Worth, Texas, for twenty-two years and my former co-laborer for twelve years, taught me a valuable and much-needed lesson. Dr. Harris said, "Harry, when I come to the end of a day and I have other things not done, I simply say: 'Lord, I tried,' and that's all you can do or all he would ask." Every minister of education will have to learn to say, "Lord, I tried."

6. He Is an Educator

While the minister of education will be involved in many duties beyond religious education, that remains and should remain his primary area of work. He should have a philosophy of religious education. He should know the educational process: *How does learning take place? When is teaching effective?* How can he lead others if he does not himself know? Often ministers of education say they spend only a handful of their time as educators. Somehow, someway we must avoid falling into that trap. The minister of education must never forget that the major area of concern is in education.

To be of maximum effectiveness in his God-called ministry, the minister of education should seek all the preparation and training possible. The minister of education should seek to attend college and seminary. He may attend any one of six Southern Baptist theological seminaries. They are as follows: Golden Gate Baptist Theological Seminary in Mill Valley, California; Midwestern Baptist Theological Seminary in Kansas City, Missouri; New Orleans Baptist Theological Seminary in New Orleans, Louisiana; Southeastern Baptist Theological Seminary in Wake Forest, North Carolina; Southern Baptist Theological Seminary in Louisville, Kentucky; and Southwestern Baptist Theological Seminary in Fort Worth, Texas.

Let it be clearly stated that while it is preferable and desirable to attend seminary, one can serve as a minister of education even if he has had no formal training. Some of our finest men have never attended seminary. It is significant, though, that most of them are quick to say, "Get your training; attend college and seminary. It will aid you immeasurably."

College and seminary training are only a beginning, however. Reginald McDonough writes, "Many persons are saying that the primary purpose of seminary education is to prepare a person for the first five years of ministry. Beyond this point a person must look to continuing education resources." [5] In addition one must read avidly. There is no way to stay current without reading. The minister of education must read periodicals, both Christian and secular.

The minister of education can, with great profit, participate in one of the five religious education associations. The Southern Baptist Religious Education Association meets annually before the Southern Baptist Convention. The Western Religious Education Association meets in a West Coast city; the Southwestern Baptist Religious Education Association meets at Southwestern Seminary in Fort Worth; the Eastern meets at Ridgecrest; and the Midwestern meets at Midwestern Seminary in Kansas City. Other similar associations are listed in *The Work of the Minister of Education,* published by Convention Press.

Some of the finest training opportunities for the minister of education and his people are the leadership training weeks at Ridgecrest Baptist Conference Center in North Carolina and at Glorieta Baptist Conference Center in New Mexico. The Church Program

Training Center at Nashville, Tennessee, also offers valuable training through the year.

Opportunities for educational training are absolutely limitless,
and one must avail himself frequently of those opportunities.

7. He Is a Student of the Word

The minister of education must be an educator. Yes! The point
has been made. But what kind of educator? A Christian educator.
Ah, there is the crux of the matter. Ministers of education are
often better known for their skill and knowledge in education than
for their skill and knowledge in the Bible and in theology. Yet if
one is skilled in education but not in Scripture, how can he be a
skilled *Christian* educator? I submit that here is a weakness which
Christian educators must recognize, acknowledge, and correct. If
the truth hurts, it is no less the truth. How can we correct this
weakness?

First, we must take the time, whatever else we neglect, to study
the Word. We must get into it. There is no substitute for regular,
consistent Bible study for ministers of education or anyone else.
Studying the Word is not reading it devotionally, though devotional
reading is good and essential. Studying it is working at it, getting
into it, becoming absorbed in it.

Second, ministers of education should take no less education
courses in seminary but additional courses in theology. This approach would add time to formal training, but it is of fundamental
importance. Ministers of education can be and often are excellent
teachers of the Word. Some are highly gifted and can speak with
a great degree of effectiveness. The more adequate the preparation,
the greater the service to the Lord and his church. A minister of
education who knows the Bible and is able to teach and speak
publicly from time to time is highly respected by his people and
is thus enabled to do a greater work for the Lord.

Even more important is the fact that the minister of education
must be a student of the Bible and theology because he is a teacher
of teachers. He is an equipper of equippers. He must have the

knowledge and training to give help where and when it is needed. He can give greater help to his workers when he has greater educational, biblical, and theological knowledge.

8. He Is a Man of Prayer

Even as the minister of education must be a student of the Word, so must he be a man of prayer. There is absolutely nothing that will take the place of regular communion with God.

Prayer is fundamental in both the Old and New Testaments. The Psalter is a rich collection of prayers of many and various kinds. The New Testament records that Jesus often prayed (Matt. 14:23; Luke 5:16; 9:18), and he taught his disciples to pray (Matt. 6:9). The early church prayed (Acts 1:24; 4:31). Paul's epistles are filled with examples of Paul's praying heart and life.

If the minister of education is to lead his people to pray, he must pray. If he is to go deeper with his Lord, he must pray. He should have a regular daily time of prayer. He will have to fight for that time because countless interruptions, activities, and persons will seem to intervene and cause delay or neglect. To be sure, the minister of education may even substitute activity and schedule for prayer, however unintentionally. He will do so only at great peril, however. When one neglects that essential discipline of the Christian life, prayer, he is always less than he could and should be in his Christian life and in his capacity as a leader.

9. He Is a Person of Integrity

Our nation today is in a precarious and unique position. Perhaps never before in our two-hundred-year history have we known such jeopardy. While some think danger is from *without,* I believe that our greatest danger lies from *within.* We have compromised our morals and cast away basic values. This action has occurred in our highest leadership on local, state, and national levels. Even some religious and Christian leaders have fallen.

These developments magnify the need for the minister of education to be a person of integrity. He must be who he says he is.

He is called of God. His life must witness to that calling. People will respect and follow one of purpose, character, and integrity. The churches must lead the way, and the minister of education is in the vanguard. Christian integrity implies truth, fairness, and justice to all persons in all cases.

10. He Is One Who Perseveres

The minister of education must persevere. No matter what comes, he must "hang in there." He will not accomplish all his goals in a week, a month, a year, or even years!

No matter what defeats, disappointments, or discouragements come, he must stay in the battle. He will have ample opportunity to be disappointed. He must not succumb but must ever keep his eyes on the call, the challenge, and especially on the Savior. The wise minister of education follows the example of Paul, who wrote, "Therefore, having this ministry by the mercy of God, we do not lose heart" (2 Cor. 4:1, RSV).

11. He Is a Manager of Time

Though the minister of education is an indefatigable worker, that is not sufficient. He must know how to manage the time God has entrusted to him. It is a priceless resource. He has more than he can do by himself, and he will have more than he and his fellow staff members can ever do together.

Mark Short writes, "One of the difficulties in time management for the minister of education is the complex nature of his task. Many different hats are worn by this valuable staff member. He is asked to accomplish a multitude of jobs, many of which are totally unrelated." [6] This fact simply points up and underscores the significance of the wisest use of time and suggests that ministers of education should "become better time managers and work smarter, not harder." [7] Mark Short's chapter on "Improving Time Management" in the book *The Work of the Minister of Education* is an especially fine treatment of this important point.

II. What He Does

Some say a minister of education is "jack of all trades and master of none." Perhaps many ministers of education would readily agree. Few places of leadership demand such varied duties and responsibilities. The minister of education may feel he is "all things to all people." In a sense that is true. He must be a generalist rather than a specialist, though he will, of course, be more effective in some areas than others.

The minister of education is at times organizer; planner; manager; supervisor.

At other times he is communicator; writer; teacher; educator.

And again, he is program leader; counselor; building superintendent; financial manager.

Often he is all of these, part of these, or none of these. Yet in it all and through it all he can be the glue that holds the work together; or he can be the irritant that keeps it from coming together. Whoever he is and whatever he does, he and his work cannot be hidden. It is for all to see and judge. His task is both frightening and challenging; it is both frustrating and fulfilling; but at all times it is significant and vital to the ongoing work of the church.

1. He Is Often Church Program Leader

A minister of education is frequently program leader in his church. Sometimes he is assigned the responsibility. Often it just works out that way. "Program leader" means one who gives leadership and direction to the various programs or organizations of the church.

If the minister of education is program leader, he, along with the pastor, gives leadership to the church council—which consists of the leaders of the church programs such as Sunday School, Church Training, WMU, Brotherhood, and Music.

As program leader he has a significant responsibility. Developing the program of a church includes creative thinking and group planning. In essence, the program is what the church intends to do in response to the commission of our Lord. It is exceedingly important that the minister of education work with each program leader and each program organization. He must leave none outside his concern. In this respect he must exercise skills in administration, coordination, and delegation.

He is directly involved with the council in setting goals, determining priorities, and establishing programs and a calendar which reflect those goals and plans.

2. He Gives Direction to the Sunday School

The minister of education must give priority leadership to the Sunday School. This organization has the greatest resources and persons with which and with whom he will work. He must spend more time with the Sunday School than any other program. To think he must spend equal time with all would be to jeopardize all. When the Sunday School prospers, all prosper. When the Sunday School does not prosper, others usually do not. Let me hasten to add, however, that the minister of education should and will work with all organizations of the church.

As the minister of education works with the Sunday School, he is responsible for leading in the development of a corps of trained and equipped leaders and teachers. He is, in fact, a trainer of trainers or an equipper of equippers. These teachers and leaders must be enlisted before they are trained. Enlistment, too, is his job. He is, of course, not to do it all; but he must see that it is done. Paul said to Timothy, "What you have heard from me before many witnesses entrust to faithful men who will be able to teach others also" (2 Tim. 2:2, RSV). So the minister of education will train teachers and leaders, and they in turn will train their class officers and members. The circle will be made, and the gospel story will go forward around the world.

The minister of education has many resources from which to choose in this training process. He will find the Church Study Course to be of great value. In addition, in the fall of 1977, the

Sunday School Board produced and marketed some of our finest training materials to date. Every church and minister of education should seek to secure some or all of the following teaching/learning improvement materials: (1) *How to Improve Bible Teaching and Learning in Sunday School: Pastor-Director Guide;* (2) *Sunday School Worker Appreciation Certificate;* (3) "You In Bible Study Now"—a pamphlet containing the answers to various questions which a Sunday School member may ask; (4) "How to Conduct Sunday School Age-Group Workers' Meetings: Training Kit"; (5) "How to Conduct Sunday School Age-Group Workers' Meetings: Response Manual"; (6) "The Teaching-Learning Improvement Package"; (7) *Training Potential Sunday School Workers;* (8) "Workers' Meeting Resource Kit." Also, teaching books are available for workers with each of the age groups. Teaching books are supported by resource kits, personal learning kits, and response manuals. High quality 16mm and videoteaching films have been produced and are available for the age divisions.

In my opinion the single greatest aid to the minister of education in his training efforts is the weekly workers' meeting. One hour and fifteen minutes per week for fifty-two weeks invested in this meeting will produce untold benefits and rewards for teachers, leaders, pupils, and ultimately for the church and the kingdom of God. A minister of education cannot and should not try to do all things; but he chooses well and wisely if he will invest a large portion of his time in seeing that his church has a functioning and effective weekly workers' meeting. Effective meetings are possible and are a reality in many churches. This achievement should be happening in countless churches across our land.

The minister of education is directly related to and responsible for the outreach of his church, since he gives direction to the Sunday School. While some churches use other organizations and programs to spearhead outreach, it is difficult to see any organization so uniquely suited to outreach as is the Sunday School. It has the greatest number of constituents, and it has more leaders and potential witnesses. The Sunday School is here to stay. The minister of education can lead his church to reach out to the lost, the confused, the bewildered, and the uninterested; and he can do it best through the Sunday School.

As the minister of education works with the Sunday School, he is not only developing a training program and a program of outreach; but he is involved in a program of Bible teaching that has unparalleled opportunities and challenges. There is more interest and concern in Bible study today than the writer has ever known before. There are many groups giving attention to Bible study, but none can do it with greater effectiveness than the Sunday School.

3. He Guides the Church Training Program

The program of Church Training offers untold opportunities. While great strides have been made in the past in church training, there are greater days ahead. The minister of education should work with the church training program in leading his people to study and learn of Christian theology, Christian ethics, Christian history, and church polity and organization. Church members need training in how to share their witness, how to minister, and how to apply their faith and live the Christian life.

In addition, new Christians and new church members need immediate training, while teachers and leaders for the various organizations must have specialized leader training. Christians are never full-grown; so there will always be a vital place for Christian training in a fellowship of believers.

Training of church members goes well beyond Sunday night training and includes weekday training such as retreats, seminars, and conferences. Weekday training can be a highly effective time for fruitful training.

4. He Works with the WMU and Brotherhood Program

Because of the amount of the work load, the minister of education may allow these two programs to go almost unnoticed. This should not be the case. The mission challenge and opportunities of a church are of deepest significance. They deserve careful and prayerful attention from the minister of education. He should have regular conferences with the leaders of these organizations. He should aid them in the enlistment and training of their workers and should work carefully with them in the development of the mission program of the church.

5. He Works with Church Committees

In most churches the minister of education spends considerable time and effort working with church committees. He works with the committee on committees to enlist committee members and write committee descriptions. He is also involved with committee meetings and follow-up reports. Southern Baptist churches do much of their work through committees; therefore, the minister of education has a vital relationship in this area. He should learn how to conduct effective committee meetings and train others in that ability. No committees should be formed or continued which have no basis in need.

6. He Works with the Deacons

While the minister of education does not usually have a direct responsibility with the deacons of the church, he does often work with them. Normally he attends the deacons' meetings and gives an educational report to them. Since deacons serve as Sunday School teachers, Church Training leaders, and/or committee members, there is a natural rapport between them and the minister of education.

When a pastor is called to a new field, the relationship of the deacons and minister of education becomes even more important. In this critical time in a church's life, they must work side by side in harmony and purpose. Too, deacons should be and often are spiritual leaders in a church. The minister of education exercises wisdom and good judgment as he counsels with them, spends time in witnessing with them, and seeks to lead them to ever-increasing growth, development, and service.

7. He Works with Church Properties

Often the minister of education has responsibility for the supervision of those who work with church properties—land, buildings, and equipment. The area of church properties is critical because it is the area the members and general public first see. It is also an area in which the minister of education usually has little special training and often feels even less calling. Even so, the needs of the work frequently require great gaps of his time. The work must be assigned; job descriptions must be written; custodial and maintenance personnel and employees must be hired and trained. Their work must be directed and supervised. The minister of education must do all that he can in this area, but he must delegate as much as possible in order that he may concentrate on the educational aspects of his task. The pastor and members of the church need special sensitivity to this fact. Otherwise, the minister of education will be unable to function effectively as a Christian educator.

8. He Works with Church Finance

The minister of education is frequently involved in the financial affairs of a church. If the church does not have a business manager, he simply cannot avoid working on finances. Finances will require a large amount of his time. He will work closely with the finance committee in the development of the church budget and in the promotion and pledging of that budget. He will work with them also in the disbursement and reporting of funds.

As in property management, the minister of education will probably have scant training or experience in this important and time-consuming area; therefore, he must wisely share with lay members and staff in all that is possible.

9. He Is Office Manager

Someone must function as office manager in a church with multiple office personnel. Who will do it? Sometimes a business administrator or other staff member has the responsibility; but most often the minister of education does so. Someone must see that job descriptions are written and that personnel policies are prepared and followed. Office workers must have direction, coordination, and supervision. Who will provide this help? In most churches it will be the minister of education, whose preparation includes very little in office management. Happily, our seminaries are beginning to offer more help in this area.

10. He Works with Food Services

The minister of education is also frequently involved in administration and supervision of the food service operation of the church. Depending on the size of the church, this assignment means another one to five persons with whom he must work. His responsibilities in this area are much the same as in the properties area.

11. He Is Writer

The minister of education will almost certainly have writing assignments which he must perform or assign to another. He may be the editor of the local church publication plus additional inside communication organs. Often he is asked to contribute to Convention periodicals. The minister of education is sometimes the public relations member of the staff. Newspapers will frequently accept well-written articles and pictures concerning the church and its program and activities. He must learn to assign some of this work load.

12. He Is Counselor

Counseling can become a major time consumer for the minister of education. If he gets deeply involved with the people with whom he serves, they will have problems and will go to him for advice and counsel. Because of his daily contact with people, these opportunities can become so numerous as to cause considerable frustration to a minister of education who really cares for his people. He will find himself counseling leaders in the church with respect to their leadership positions. This is a natural and proper area of counseling for him. When he becomes involved in counseling those who have deep emotional problems, he should be aware of referral agencies in his community.

13. He Is Minister

The minister of education often is assigned a day to visit in the hospitals; or if not, he has the responsibility and privilege of ministry to the ones with whom he serves closely. Of course, this relationship is always discussed with the pastor. I have found great satisfaction from a ministry with those who hurt. Many ministers of education are ordained and often conduct funerals and weddings in the church. This relationship is always carefully structured with the pastor.

Should a minister of education be ordained? Nearly all biblical scholars believe ordination is right and scriptural for all the ministers in our churches, whether they are ministers of education, ministers of music, or pastors. Even so, some ministers of education adhere to the traditional principle that only pastors of churches are ordained and, therefore, prefer not to be ordained. Most, however, probably prefer ordination.

I have heard the suggestion that ministers of education should be ordained in order to receive the rights and privileges of ordination such as income tax allowances. Absolutely not. That factor should have nothing to do with ordination to the gospel ministry. Such a practice is foreign to the spirit of Christ.

14. He Is Personal Witness

A ministry that must not be neglected no matter what the size of the church or the number of staff members is that of personal visitation, which includes witnessing to the unsaved and to the unchurched. The quickest way for a minister of education to "dry up" is to neglect personal witnessing. The greatest undertaking God has laid out is to lead persons to Jesus.

No one has ever been successful in leading people to do that which he was unwilling to do. Never has this been more true than in witnessing. Nothing is more important or more neglected. One's own caring and concern for the lost and uninterested is always in direct proportion to the frequency with which he attempts to witness. There is no excuse for any minister of education to neglect this area of his work. He will never do anything of greater significance.

15. He Works with Community Agencies

The minister of education should have a working and practical knowledge of community resources. He should know how, when, and where to refer persons who have physical, emotional, and social needs that he is unable to meet. Nearly every community provides a handbook or manual that carefully describes most helping agencies of the city.

Too, he should be acquainted with Christian counselors and psychiatrists when the occasion requires it. Certainly, I do not suggest that the church fail or cease to minister in these areas. Indeed, it should and does minister. There are times, however, when the church should guide persons to specialists in certain areas.

16. He Works with Other Baptist Groups

The minister of education will find much assistance from the local association, state convention, and the Southern Baptist Convention. Not only is help provided for him and his church, but he has a responsibility to assist Southern Baptist groups as they seek to give guidance to the churches of our Convention. He should be willing to take his turn as an officer when called upon and to lead conferences and workshops from time to time. He has received much from Southern Baptists; he has the privilege and responsibility of returning a portion.

The reader may be wondering at this point how one person can accomplish all of these responsibilities. Is it really that way for all ministers of education? Of course not. Clarification should be made at this point. Surely few ministers of education will read this chapter and say, "That describes my task to a 'T!' " The reason is obvious: Ministers of education serve in varying sizes of churches and staffs. Some churches have only a pastor, minister of education, and secretary. Others have multiple pastors, education staff, secretaries, and other employees. The position taken here is that one who is considering the field of minister of education could find in this chapter some understanding of what a minister of education is and what he would do. Or a minister of education in a large church could identify with what is written while recognizing that it may not exactly describe his situation.

In the July 7, 1977, "Shoreliner" of the First Baptist Church, Corpus Christi, Texas, there appeared the job description for their new minister of education. It is shared here to demonstrate a fairly typical description of the work of a minister of education:

"He will give general supervision to the religious education program of the church.

"He will give direction to the outreach ministries of the church, such as visitation, Bible study groups, Vacation Bible Schools, International Club, bus ministries, and such other innovative programs as he may devise.

"The minister of education will supervise the Day School program, working closely with the Day School Committee and with the director of the Day School.

"The minister of education will give direction to the promotion of good stewardship in the congregation and subscribing of the annual budget.

"The minister of education will act as office manager, supervising the secretaries and authorizing the purchase of supplies.

"The building superintendent and the church hostess will report to the minister of education.

"The minister of education will be public relations director for the church and will be responsible for advertising, brochures, and other means of getting the church before the community.

"Other responsibilities may accrue as the needs arise and upon consultation with the pastor."

III. WHAT HIS SPECIAL RELATIONSHIPS ARE

If a minister of education serves a church with 500, 1,000, 5,000, or 10,000 members, he cannot work with each member individually no matter how hard he tries or how badly he wants to do so. It simply cannot be done. Since he cannot work closely with each one, it follows he has to work closely with some. Who are they?

From twenty-five years of experience in the field of religious education in the local church, I have the conviction that some key relationships are absolutely essential if the minister of education is to do his job effectively.

1. He Has a Unique Relationship with the Pastor

First and foremost is the relationship with the pastor. There is no substitute for a harmonious and happy relationship with the pastor. That is where it all begins. A minister of education may get along well with everyone except the pastor, and the seeds of failure are already present. Nor is that failure always the pastor's fault. There are some suggestions for the minister of education in his relationship with the pastor:

First, the minister of education must recognize that he is not the pastor. He is not the primary leader of the church. That is and should be the pastor's role. The minister of education need not think that he is inferior or that his place of service is inferior. When one is doing God's will, he is never in an inferior position. There is no place of greater service than in the center of God's will.

Second, the minister of education should never "run ahead" of his pastor. He should seek his counsel and ask his advice, especially on things new or different. Most ministers of education do not like surprises; neither do pastors. The pastor can be adviser, confidant, and counselor to the minister of education.

The other side of the coin should be viewed also. The pastor is not dictator; nor is the minister of education vassal. The pastor should allow the minister of education to do his work with considerable freedom and initiative. It is to his advantage and the advantage of the church. The minister of education can lengthen immeasurably the "arms of the pastor" if he is allowed to function.

Third, the minister of education and the pastor should regularly communicate with each other. They must discuss problems and needs and commit them to prayer. They should occasionally visit together in witnessing opportunities. Pastor and minister of education can, should be, and frequently are not only co-laborers but the warmest and dearest of friends. Some of my finest relationships have been with my four pastors. I count them as close and dear friends to this day.

Fourth, and perhaps most important, let the minister of education and pastor seek to know as much as possible about each other *before* they serve on the same church staff. Since the minister of education will have no more important relationship than with his pastor, let him come to know the pastor by spending long hours with him, asking questions, and probing the relationship. What is most important to the pastor? What are his goals? How does he work with people? What kind of leader is he? What does he expect of the minister of education? Points of agreement and disagreement need to be determined before the relationship becomes a reality. Be open, frank, and honest. It will pay great dividends. There is no sweeter relationship than when the hearts, minds, and spirits of pastor and minister of education are together.

2. He Has a Special Relationship with the Staff

No minister of education will see the greatest possible fruit from his labor until he has satisfactory relationships with all the members of the staff. He will not feel the same way about each one. He should not. Each is different. God made them that way. Yet he must see each as an important member of the team. If one hurts, all hurt. If one experiences joy, all can experience joy.

As with the pastor, communication is not just important; it is absolutely fundamental. Staff members must see each other, talk to each other, and pray with and for each other. Let them cease talking and praying with each other, and difficulties and problems are not far behind.

Often the minister of education gives direction to a church staff. If so, the team concept in staff relations is a tried, tested, and proven one. The minister of education will do well to see himself as one who guides, assists, counsels, and seeks in every way to aid each member of the team. Churches that move forward and make progress for the kingdom usually do so together as a team.

To achieve team spirit and desired results, individual conferences with staff members are necessary from time to time. Weekly meetings with the staff as a whole are invaluable. One- to two-day staff retreats are profitable for good communication and planning. While time can be wasted with too-numerous meetings, careful planning and structuring of agenda will lessen that possibility.

3. He Has a Special Relationship with Church Program Leaders

The minister of education should give attention and time to all the church program leaders. The work of the church goes on through their leadership. He must confer with them in enlistment of leaders and development of program. He must relate to them in special events and opportunities.

I have found that a scheduled time with program leaders once a month is minimal. The minister of education must find time to spend with those who are responsible for the program organizations of the church. Of course, the church council relationship is highly productive.

4. He Has a Special Relationship with Sunday School and Church Training Directors

No minister of education can build a Sunday School or a Church Training Program. No lay Sunday School or Church Training director can do it. No pastor can do it alone. But a great Sunday School and Church Training program can be built! Great Sunday Schools and training programs in America are being built now, and there will be more in the future. As a minister of education, I have found that I cannot work with each teacher and leader in each department, not even in the smallest Sunday School in which I served. That is not to say that I did not want to or that I did not try; but it is best done by working through the department directors in Sunday School and Church Training.

How can this be done? Visit in each department director's home or talk with him at church; have a weekly directors' meeting if at all possible. Cultivate the directors; give them good books; encourage them; praise them; love them; depend on them; believe in them. Department directors will respond and work and pray, and God will produce miracles through them. They will grow and develop as he wants them to. Remember that you cannot work closely with each one, but you can work closely with some.

5. He Has an Indispensable Relationship with His Family

It may appear unusual to list family as a special relationship, but I believe it is more than special. A happy family relationship is absolutely essential to effective, fulfilling, and enduring work as a minister of education. It is indeed a sad and tragic fact that many church staff leaders are faced with major family problems. It is probably easier for a minister of education to neglect his immediate family than it is to neglect persons or groups in the church. The neglect may be an insidious thing. It may creep up on him without his realizing it, but it will always be costly neglect for whatever the reason. While some may sincerely believe that family can be neglected when "the Lord's work" is being performed, I most certainly do not. There is not a shred of scriptural evidence to support that belief or practice. The relationship of the minister of education with his family takes precedence over his relationship with the church.

The minister of education must spend time with each individual member of his family, and he must spend time with his family members together. Good family relationships require love, patience, communication, understanding, and, above all, *time* for these attributes to develop. Most church members want the minister of education to give proper time and attention to his family relationships. He is a stronger and better leader because of those effective relationships. Whatever it means in his personal and church schedule, he must make the adjustments to make certain that he does not neglect his own family while ministering to others.

IV. What He Can Expect to Receive

The minister of education who is called of God does not serve for rewards—but he will most certainly receive some.

First, doing God's will is one of the greatest satisfactions that life offers; and it is one of life's greatest achievements. Just the "doing of his will" is reward enough—but there is more.

Second, the minister of education can know and will discover that he serves in the greatest cause on earth. To be a vital part of sharing the gospel with the world is a grand and glorious experience. There is none like it. The cause is eminently worthwhile. It is rewarding beyond one's highest dreams.

Third, the minister of education who loves his people will find that love returned a hundredfold. He will receive far more than he can ever give. No matter what his salary, he will be highly paid. To love and to be loved and appreciated is one of life's greatest experiences.

Fourth, the minister of education will find that his work is bigger than he is. It is exciting and challenging. It will call forth the best that he has. Everyone needs a challenge beyond himself.

To those who consider the field of religious education, I say, Study, think, and pray; the field is truly "white unto harvest." There is room for you. You have a challenging opportunity and a task bigger than you; but it is worth your life. Come on in; join us!

To those who are new ministers of education, I say, "Welcome! God loves you." How good to count you in our number. You are in a great crowd who will love and help you. Your life as a minister of education has challenge, thrill, excitement, and achievement ahead.

To those "veterans" in the field, I say thank you for giving our

Lord and his church your best all these years. You have your reward, and I have mine. Isn't God good to trust us with so great a place of service!

Notes

1. J. Oswald Sanders, *Spiritual Leadership* (Chicago: Moody Press, 1967), p. 13.

2. Ibid.

3. Les Giblin, *How to Have Confidence and Power in Dealing with People* (New York: Prentice-Hall, Inc., 1956), p. 4.

4. Lawrence A. Appley, *Management in Action* (New York: American Management Association, 1956), p. 18.

5. Will Beal, comp., *The Work of the Minister of Education* (Nashville: Convention Press, 1976), p. 106.

6. Ibid., p. 75.

7. Ibid.

3.
The Minister of Education and Music

This chapter deals with an assignment that has a unique dimension. Two distinct areas of the ministry of religious education have been combined into a single job description: minister of education and music.

Is there a biblical precedent for a minister with a combination position? If so, what are the unique challenges of the dual approach? What qualifications and training are necessary? How can one person adequately handle such a combination role? These and other questions will be explored in this chapter.

I. FINDING A BIBLICAL BASIS FOR THE COMBINATION MINISTER

Is there indeed a biblical precedent for the combination role in the ministry? At the risk of being called a "proof-texter," I feel that there is.

The Apostle Paul, one of the first ministers of the New Testament church, was well versed in the purposes of the church and the role of the minister. In Ephesians 4:11 he referred to the various ministries to which God calls. It is interesting to note that after listing a number of individual ministries, he concludes with a combination of two ministries as he refers to "pastors *and* teachers." There it is—probably the first indication of a combination worker in the New Testament church!

While there may be a difference in interpretation of the passage, a comparison of translations as well as evidence in other Scripture passages weighs heavily in favor of the interpretation that Paul was referring to a combination of responsibilities performed by one person.

II. DETERMINING PRIORITIES AS A COMBINATION MINISTER

"Just one final question, Mr. Robinson." Mr. Stone, the chairman of the church personnel committee, was speaking. "If our church should call you as minister of education and music, what would your priority be?"

I cleared my throat to answer. The answer would be easy—or would it? "Mr. Chairman," I began, "my preference would be . . ." For some reason I hesitated. All of my professional life I had known what field of specialization I would claim if the Lord should lead.

But suddenly I realized that my response was not the answer to Mr. Stone's question. He had not asked for my preference, but for my priority. This question I was not prepared to answer. It sent me mentally scurrying for a response. Soon my mind went to Matthew 28:19-20, Christ's commission to his church. If it were Christ's priority, it must be mine as his servant.

For the first time it was clear that my priority could not be music or education, but rather the New Testament commission to reach, teach, win, and develop people for Christ. Music and education programs would be merely tools through which I would seek to lead the church to accomplish these New Testament priorities.

To be sure, serving through the dual disciplines of education and music does make unique demands upon the individual. But once acceptance of the priority established in the Bible is a reality, combining areas of ministry becomes easier to handle.

III. QUALIFYING AS A MINISTER OF EDUCATION AND MUSIC

How does a person qualify as a combination minister? In every field of endeavor there are qualities and aptitudes which enhance a person's ability to perform successfully in his chosen field. Particularly is this true of the combination minister. There are nine basic qualifications that are important to the combination minister.

1. Be a God-Called Person

"Here am I, send me" (Isa. 6:8), was the way Isaiah expressed the dedication he felt toward God. "I make available to you, Lord, all that I am," he seemed to be saying. Such a spirit of submission must be at the heart of a commitment to the ministry of education and music.

The call to the combination ministry is a unique and demanding one. An inward confidence that the combined ministry of education and music is God's place for a person is of utmost importance. Anything less is unlikely to stand the tests of time and the demands of the position.

The matter of divine call is discussed in detail in an earlier chapter. The reader is urged to review it for a fuller treatment of the subject.

2. Be a "Galatian"-type Christian

In Galatians 5:22 Paul related some attributes he considered essential to the Christian. If they are important to the Christian, they are doubly important to persons who lead Christians. Paul's list includes patience, love, joy, goodness, faithfulness, gentleness, and self-control.

Because these qualities are not basic to human nature, they must be cultivated. Through regular Bible study and through prayer to the giver of these gifts, these qualities cannot only strengthen one's personal relationship, but will even influence the style of leadership.

Results in education and music work can sometimes be extremely slow and tedious. The "Galatian" life-style as Paul proposed it will serve the minister of education and music well as he ministers to the church under a variety of circumstances.

3. Be a Team Member

An extremely successful football coach was the guest of a church. During a question-and-answer period which followed his scheduled speech, he was asked what he considered to be the most important qualification for a member of his football team. His answer was immediate and direct: the right attitude! He then went on to relate this attribute specifically to a player's attitude toward fellow team members.

A church staff is not unlike a football team. Each member must see himself as a part of a team if he and the team are to find success. The goal of the minister of education and music—to reach, teach, win, and develop people for Christ and his church—is the same as that of every other member of the staff team. Only the position he plays in the fulfillment of that goal is different.

4. Have a Love for People

The ministry of education and music is "people business." The programs are the tools used in ministering to the needs of the people.

If a staff member loves the people with whom he works, he will have gone a long way toward achieving success as a minister. He must love them as they are. He must love them when they are unlovable. He must love them for what they can become for Christ. Most of the people may *respect* a minister for his knowledge and skill, but almost all of them will *respond* to the love the staff member has for them as individuals.

5. Have an Aptitude and Appreciation for Music

Up to this point the qualifications have related specifically to people. It is time for consideration of one of the tools of ministry.

It is obvious that the person who aspires to minister through music must be a lover of music. He must believe in the power of music to inspire and transform the lives of the people.

Because music is a highly specialized art, a certain degree of aptitude is essential. Experience shows that the music program will reach no greater heights than those to which the minister of music can lead. The minister of education and music must not only have a thorough academic background in music; he must continue to study and prepare with great diligence.

6. Be Apt to Lead

If the combination minister is to cover all of the bases of a comprehensive education and music program, he must be a strong leader who believes in using and developing the persons with whom he works. Strong leadership begins with an adequate philosophy of leadership. In general there are two possible philosophies. They are closely related, but they are also quite diverse in character. They are the *quarterback* philosophy and the *coach* philosophy.

The *quarterback* staffer is a star performer. He considers it important to be in on every play. He finds it hard to delegate plays to other team members. He sets up the plays and will run the play with the slightest provocation. He may talk about using others, but he has difficulty in letting go of the ball long enough to let someone else run a play.

The *coach* staff person is no less involved in the game, but he works from an entirely different vantage point. He utilizes his skill by conducting pregame sessions with the team. He is a familiar sight along the sidelines as he counsels and encourages his team on to victory. His game plan, then, is to exert leadership through training, motivating, and group planning strategies. His plan is detailed, and he communicates it well to his team.

The coach-type leader is an enabler. His personal position with the team is strengthened because he has strengthened its individual members. They rise up to call him blessed for his influence on their personal Christian growth.

Experience leads to the conclusion that the latter plan is not only the wiser choice, but the *only* way the combination minister can accomplish his multifaceted task.

7. Be Sensitive to Others

Persons who serve in staff positions in a church are called upon almost daily to deal with potentially difficult situations. A tactful person who is sensitive to the needs and feelings of others can be used of God to calm many troublesome waters. His sensitivity to the needs of others is expressed in his making judgments only after all of the facts are in. He can strengthen his leadership position by not making an issue of every situation. Such Christian sensitivity develops the confidence of the people in the leader and makes them more likely to follow his leadership.

8. Develop a Sense of Humor

Have you ever been in a group meeting where tension seemed to be mounting by the minute? Suddenly something humorous was said by the leader; perhaps a humorous story was told. Remember how everyone laughed? When it was over, everyone was relaxed and a good spirit prevailed. Looking back, it seemed that this tension breaker was the turning point in the meeting. This illustration is just one example of how important a sense of humor is for the leader.

The ability to laugh at oneself can also relieve personal tensions and tensions within a group. It can also keep one's judgments in perspective. Everyone makes mistakes, but the person who can laugh at his own foibles will win friends and gain the confidence of the people he leads.

9. Be Able to Adjust

Ministers who have come up in the midtwentieth century know about change. In every area of life they have been affected by change—and more change. Leaders should know what is right and stand by their decisions, but at the same time they need to be able and willing to make changes when the occasion demands. The minister of education and music who learns early to adjust to situations he cannot immediately change will not only have a happier tenure where he serves, but he will ultimately make a difference with the people where he serves.

IV. Equipping for Maximum Service

"You've had a long and useful career," I said to my minister of music and education friend. His graying temples and furrowed forehead bore testimony to his maturing years. The strength of the churches he had served spoke eloquently of his effectiveness as a combination man. "To what," I asked him, "do you attribute your success as a combination man?"

I listened intently as he responded thoughtfully, for I valued his judgment. "If I've achieved any measure of success in my field, it's because I determined at the time I was called into Christian service to equip myself for the task. The rest I've left to God."

His were words of wisdom which need to be repeated often. The commitment of the combination man must involve a commitment to excellence—in both fields.

1. Where the Equipping Begins

Proper equipping for ministry begins with a divine call. Although the subject has been discussed amply under previous topics, its significance demands that it be at the top of any discussion of equipping for ministry.

2. The Equipping Continues

Teacher—leader—vocalist—vocal pedagogist—administrator—counselor—program planner—coordinator—choral conductor—organizer—motivator. Each of these roles brings a nod of recognition to the combination minister, for they are areas in which he deals every day. Such diversity of ministry demands diversity of preparation.

How does the minister of education and music become qualified to be an equipper? Hopefully, it will begin with on-the-job training in the local church long before his formal education begins. If he has had music training in his youth, that will be helpful. If not, certainly he will want to make music training a matter for strong concentration when he attends college and seminary. A degree in music from an accredited college will be an imperative.

There is no question but that it will be wise for this person to continue his education at a Southern Baptist seminary. There he will find advanced degrees available in religious education and in music. Most seminaries now make available a combination degree which gives equal emphasis to training in both disciplines.

The combination degree often receives only slight consideration by some students because it means an extra year or two of seminary-level work. However, any person who feels any call or interest in the combination work should avoid the temptation to sell himself short by taking the shorter route, which results in preparation in only one field. If seminary training is impossible or if the minister's call comes late in life, he can to some degree overcome his handicap by studying with the Southern Baptist Seminary Extension Department of the Southern Baptist Convention.

3. The Equipping Culminates

It is often said that the graduate launching a career today will have to be retrained two or three times during his lifetime. The combination minister is not likely to be an exception to this rule. Any mature minister will verify that many of the terms, tools, and techniques that he uses today were not even in existence when he entered his chosen field thirty, twenty, or even fifteen years ago. Lifelong preparation is especially important to the combination minister. To stand still is to lose ground in this dynamic ministry.

Many opportunities are available to the combination person to continue his professional growth. Glorieta and Ridgecrest Baptist Conference Centers, in New Mexico and North Carolina respectively, are located in scenic terrain which is conducive to a renewal in a relaxed learning environment. Both centers offer periodic training on a year-round basis.

Short-term seminars sponsored by The Sunday School Board of the Southern Baptist Convention at its Church Program Training

Center in Nashville offer excellent opportunity for updating one's skills.

The developing concept of continuing education for the local church minister of education and music is a plan that has been practiced in other fields for many years. The sabbatical gives the minister the opportunity to sharpen his skills and renew himself spiritually through an extended period of training away from the church field. Because both church and staff benefit, this opportunity is usually provided for financially through the church budget. A sabbatical update is a concept that deserves the serious consideration of more churches.

V. Establishing Good Relationships in the Ministry

One does not have to be in the ministry of education and music long before he realizes that everything he does relates to someone else. This ministry is one of relationships. Because the way one relates to others affects directly the success one experiences, it would be well to consider briefly some of the relationships of the combination minister.

1. Relating to God

As a minister, one's first obligation is to be a consistent Christian. "But seek ye first the kingdom of God and his righteousness; and all these things shall be added unto you" (Matt. 6:33).

Only through a consistent life of prayer and Bible study can any individual develop this relationship. Until this relationship has been established, the minister is like a person seeking to return from a place where he has never been. It is futile to try to lead people to a relationship that he has not experienced personally.

2. Relating to Oneself

Until one understands himself, it is difficult to see others in proper perspective. Until one believes in himself, he has difficulty in believing in others.

Self-awareness leads to self-acceptance; and self-acceptance leads to self-giving, which is the heart of the ministry.

How can the minister of education and music know whether he has a good relationship with himself? Certain criteria will be helpful.

1. Be able to accept criticism without taking it personally.

2. Learn how to organize the work by priorities, thus keeping the ministry off the basis of simply meeting emergencies.

3. Learn the importance of keeping physically fit. Fitness not only extends one's usefulness, but it also provides a healthy outlet for frustrations.

4. Learn the importance of being personally attractive. To fail to keep one's weight under control, clothes neat and well fitted, and to be personally well groomed hints at a poor self-image and even suggests an inability to keep other areas of life under control.

5. Allocate adequate time for rest. Cavett Roberts, a nationally known motivation speaker, put it well when he said, "If you expect to fly with the eagles by day, you can't hoot with the owls at night."

6. Be willing to admit mistakes. The words "I was wrong" are difficult to muster at times; but they strengthen, not weaken, one's standing.

7. Control fear. Fear cultivates failure. To fear the unknown is a natural emotion, but it must not be allowed to control or interfere with the things that should be done.

3. Relating to One's Family

The greatest sin in relationship with one's family is probably the sin of omission, that of letting other things infringe on family time. A last-minute problem to be solved and the resulting postponement of a family plan is a devastating blow to the family relationships of the minister. Meetings and other occupational responsibilities must be handled, but family time also has priority.

The staff person is in a unique position. He relates to two God-given institutions: the church and the family (home). Both are important. Neither can be neglected.

Every staff member and every church has differing needs, so the education and music minister must deal with both church and family needs in terms of his own situation. These guidelines may be helpful:

1. Time spent with the family should be evaluated in terms of quality as well as quantity.

2. Frequent evaluation of church activities against the goals of the church helps keep meetings consistent with need.

3. Activities that give high visibility or specialize in public relations are not necessarily the best use of time. While certain meetings of a civic, church, and denominational nature are important, they too must be placed under the microscope of Bible priorities if balance and perspective are to be maintained.

4. Relating to Fellow Staff Members

Any minister who has ever been in a situation where staff relations were not of the highest type will echo the importance of the need for a good relationship. More time is spent in these relationships than in any other. The time factor alone serves to emphasize the need for a quality relationship with the total staff.

Paul indicated that the acceptance of Christ's authority is the beginning of real freedom. This principle can well be extended into the area of staff relations.

Every group must have a leader, a voice of authority. Because of his unique relationship to the church, the pastor is the one to be the leader of the staff. A basic understanding and acceptance of this fact will serve the combination staffer well. It can free him of concerns that do not rightly belong to him. It can put him in the position of majoring on things that are necessary to an effective education and music program.

Another basic principle is togetherness. The staff that prays together and plays together stays together. Staff members lead busy lives, but they should not be drawn away from the excitement of knowing each other as individuals, as people with a common purpose. Learning to relate well with each other fosters a spirit of oneness that transcends programs and lets staffers see people and church priorities as being the common cause for all.

5. Relating to the Church

The fact that church relationship is listed last in the sequence only emphasizes the fact that it is the pinnacle of relationships with which the combination staff member must deal. If other relationships are at their best, this one is more likely to be a profitable one.

Voltaire is credited with saying that "the first step which one makes is the one on which depends the rest of one's days." This concept is true of the relationship between church and staff. Certain basic understandings can spell the difference between the unhappy relationship and a happy one.

A basic agreement by the combination person and the church and pastor as to the objectives of the church is important to a harmonious relationship. Agreement should include doctrine as well as cultural considerations. In this day when segments of society would de-emphasize and divide the church, it is important that churches and staff members stand united.

A good church relationship means serving all of the people. Because a servant's heart is at the center of one's call, the minister of education and music cannot afford to serve only a part of the congregation or even a part of its organizations. A love of people will help with the relationship to the congregation. An understanding of the job description and what is expected will enhance the relationship to the organizations.

VI. Looking to the Future of the Combination Minister

In the early days of twentieth-century America there was a gentleman who was very much a part of the American scene. Wherever he went his presence was felt. He was the revered country doctor.

In his role he brought new life to the community as he delivered the babies of the young adults. Just as faithfully he served the aged and the dying. Whatever surgical procedures were required, he performed. Not one member of the family was exempt from his concern and ministry.

With the urbanization of America and the improvement of the transportation system, the country doctor or general practitioner, as he was also known, gave way to a new type of physician who practiced only in highly specialized areas.

But the final medical chapter has not been written. In recent years there has appeared on the scene a new medical phenomenon, not unlike the old general practioner. His title is different and he has a different set of credentials, but he treats the entire family as did his predecessor. He is by training and job description a specialist—a family physician.

In our Baptist churches there has been for many years a professional who has served faithfully and effectively in all areas of the religious education and music program of the churches. With the trend toward specialization the combination man has often been overlooked, as specialists of many kinds have come on the scene.

Yet all the while, requests from the churches for combination persons have been increasing. With the growth of our churches both numerically and financially, the demand for combination ministers has grown to several times that of the call for a specialist. The result is that the demand far exceeds the supply.

Southern Baptists must meet the demand for more combination workers. Like the medical profession which has made the family physician a specialist in title, training, and professional esteem, Baptists must do the same for the minister of education and music.

The need for combination workers should be interpreted to young people. They should be encouraged to give attention to equal training in each field as they prepare.

Those persons who are combination people should look upon their own call to combination work as a continuing one, rather than as a stepping-stone to some specialization at a later time.

Colleges and seminaries should strengthen the position of the combination ministry by giving it stronger emphasis and improved training opportunities.

There will always be a need for age-group and other specialists. God calls and will continue to call his people into those fields. But with the growing need for people who can serve in dual roles, pastors, churches, and schools need to actively work at emphasizing the call to combination ministries and to work toward improving the quality of training and recognition for these ministries. When these things occur, far more churches and far more ministers can render a greater service to the kingdom of God.

4.
The Minister of Adult Education

The last two decades have been a time of phenomenal growth in a large number of Southern Baptist churches. Churches that traditionally had been one- or two-staff churches were forced to rethink their staff positions. Pastors, already overloaded with preaching, pastoral, and administrative duties, could no longer give adequate leadership to the education program of the church. The need for help plunged many churches into a new era staffwise, with the creation of multiple staff roles.

I. REVIEW THE BACKGROUND OF THE POSITION OF MINISTER OF ADULT EDUCATION

Creation of the position of minister of education was the first step taken by many churches to meet the needs of rapid church membership growth. Some of the most pressing needs were and are an increasing demand for reaching the multitudes, a higher quality in the educational program, correlation of the work by various church organizations, and the enlistment and training of additional volunteer lay leaders. The emergence of these needs produced recognition of another need—specialization of leadership within the age groups as a major approach to meeting education needs.

The first step by most churches moving to multiple staff roles was to add a minister of education. However, as the responsibilities of this position grew both in administration and correlation of all the age-group work, it became evident to some churches that professional help was needed to meet the growing education demands of the age division, particularly the diversified Adult Division.

The initial approach in regrouping staff responsibilities to provide professional leadership for adult education has been to give the minister of education the responsibility for the Adult Division and to call additional staff members to work with Youth, Children, and Preschool Divisions. This regrouping is a step in the right direction.

Other churches are meeting this need for assistance in adult education by calling full-time ministers of adult education. The job description for this assignment varies. While some persons are called to work with all adults (married, single, and senior adults), others are called to work in specialized areas such as college, singles, career, young adults, and senior adults. Their titles vary from college associate to minister to singles to minister of senior adult education to singles minister.

In a letter Clois R. Smith, minister of education and adult education, Tallowood Baptist Church, Houston, Texas, said, "Churches are saying to me that they are finally recognized; they should have moved to the adult 'specialist' long ago (even before any other age group). . . . We are recognizing the need for dividing adult responsibilities re: singles, young adults, and senior adults. We now have a singles minister. We're moving toward the senior minister. With 80 percent of all prospects in this age group, we must concentrate on adults more than we have previously."

Suffice it to say that a church should consider calling a minister of adult education after prayerfully determining the need for a new position. Basic in this decision would be a concept advanced by Will Beal: "A call is not only a selection by God but also an acceptance and a commitment by the called. In a glorious way, one's call to service is a combined harmonious effort that includes: (1) God's seeking, (2) man's response, (3) the church's need." [1]

II. Develop a Philosophy of Adult Education

An adequate philosophy of adult education is basic to service as a minister of adult education. It should include accurate concepts of the role and the objective of the adult education program.

The minister of adult education is not the "program." He should be the catalyst. He helps to produce growth and change in the lives of all adults. "The task of adult education in the church is to bring the adult into a dynamic encounter that provides an interpretation of the Christian life. He [the adult] must be led to enter it through faith in Christ, and then be guided in the continued living of it." [2]

The philosophy of adult education must include provision of educational opportunities for all ages of adults—both saved and unsaved, active and inactive, and adults with usual and unusual needs. For example, there are adults who have spent their lives in the church while rearing their children. After the children leave home, some parents are ready for a "rest" from responsibility in the church. The minister of adult education faces a challenge as he seeks to meet the needs of these adults before their loss of interest in the church is permanent. Paul Bergevin substantiates this idea in his book, *A Philosophy for Adult Education,* in which he discusses the philosophy of adult education and how this philosophy puts the learner and his needs first.

III. Get an Overview of a Possible Job Description

The scope of the position of minister of adult education can be seen in the job description from South Main Baptist Church, Houston, Texas. Bob Hines presently serves this church as the capable minister of adult education.

Principal Function:

The minister of adult education is responsible to the administrator for coordinating and promoting the adult educational program.

Regular Duties:

1. Coordinate adult departments in Sunday School, Church Training, and weekday activities; recommend and implement approved promotional projects.

2. Enlist and train leadership.

3. Develop a program of fellowship, retreats, and seminars for this age group.

4. Develop goals for work with adults.

5. Lead workers in a systematic program of visitation.

6. Keep abreast of latest educational methods.

7. Prepare budget request for approval; maintain budget.

8. Preach and teach as assigned.

9. Perform other duties as assigned.

IV. BE AWARE OF THE SCOPE, DIVERSITY, AND CHALLENGE OF THE CONSTITUENCY

The adult years constitute the longest span of any age division. They comprise approximately 50 percent of the total enrollment in Sunday School and Church Training; yet adults make up the overwhelming majority of the prospects unreached by the church. Adults also have a tremendous influence in the home and in society. Adults help build all other age groups while serving as leaders. "If churches are to achieve their essential mission, they must have the leadership, resources, and influence that adults alone can provide." [3] Churches must determine to meet the challenge offered by adults today.

There is a great diversity in the adult world. It is a world of single adults, young adults, median adults, and senior adults.

With the criteria for adulthood being (1) high school graduation and up, (2) eighteen years of age and up, (3) marriage and up, the needs of adults are multiple and complex. These needs call for flexibility in the adult education program.

Included in the adult constituency are a number of special groups, all of whom the minister of adult education serves, unless responsibility is shared by another adult staff worker. These special groups of adults include the following:

Singles.—There are approximately forty million singles, nearly one out of every three adults. Included in this group are the never-married, the divorced, and the widowed.

Internationals and Language Groups.—Adults who do not speak English are sometimes concentrated in metropolitan or university areas.

Young Adults Away.—This group includes college students, military personnel, and persons who move temporarily because of employment opportunities.

Deaf adults.—Adults who cannot hear need to be included in the adult education program.

Handicapped Adults.—Trainable and educable retarded adults along with the physically handicapped are included in this special group.

Homebound Adults.—These persons are adults who are confined to their homes or institutions because of illness or age or the need to care for someone who is ill or aged.

Sunday Workers and Shift Workers.—Adults whose work schedules prevent their regular Sunday or weekday involvement make up this group.

In-service Members.—Adults who work in other age groups need the ministry of the Adult Division.

Senior Adults.—Adults sixty years of age and over should be recognized as valuable contributing members with a multiplicity of gifts and abilities. In many churches the greatest untapped source of committed resources and support is among the senior adults.

V. Understand and Cultivate Relationships Involved in the Assignment

Effective and wholesome relationships are basic factors in successful service as a minister of adult education. Without relationships there is no ministry; it is relationships upon which the ministry is founded. Therefore, an understanding of relationships is essential.

Christian love and concern for one another should be incentive enough to have good relationships. However, in working closely with someone to achieve a common goal, an extra effort should be made to seek the best relationship possible. Communication is of vital importance to ensure successful working relationships.

The minister of adult education must not only recognize the importance of relationships but also be aware of the area in which his relationships will be concentrated.

1. Relationships with Pastor

The minister of adult education must acknowledge that the pastor is the leader of the church. Both should be God-called and qualified in their chosen field.

The pastor and minister of adult education must be loyal to each other and to other members of the team. There should be an openness between the two that allows for personal and professional honesty and that enables either to state his opposing viewpoint in the presence of the other and others as well.[4]

2. Relationships with Church Staff

The minister of adult education is a member of the staff team. He should give encouragement and assistance to others with whom he works.

"A church staff is an aggregate of individuals who are brought together to achieve certain objectives in leading and being a part of a Christian congregation. How well the staff functions as a group and at the same time how well the atmosphere exists for individual fulfillment of personal needs will determine the effectiveness of staff operations." [5]

The program of the church is a total program in which every staff member must have a vital interest. Planning the work of the church together helps to prevent misunderstanding and strife. This achievement calls for regular staff meetings. "The optimum value of a staff meeting lies in the change it produces in the participants such as knowledge, attitude, behavior, and work habits." [6]

Calendar planning at each staff meeting is crucial. Annual calendar planning can be done in conjunction with the church council or at a staff and church council workshop. This planning session should be held away from the church. Adequate time should be allotted to get the job done.

The minister of adult education should find time to be with individual staff members. A racketball game, a round of golf, or lunch together can do wonders in improving staff relationships.

3. Relationships with Church Program Organization Leaders

A clear understanding of the tasks of Sunday School, Church Training, and the mission organizations is essential. The minister of adult education has special interest in and regular planning sessions with the leaders of the church program organizations. It is important that he have good working relationships with the leaders in these organizations.

4. Relationships with Volunteers

The minister of adult education works with a host of volunteers. These volunteers serve in church-elected leadership positions without remuneration. "The great army of lay leaders who give their time and talents to Christian service through church leadership positions makes up a mighty force for God. Without this work force the education, outreach, and ministry programs of churches would be reduced to a token of their present size and significance." [7]

These volunteers include department directors, teachers, class leaders, department leaders, leaders in missionary education, leaders in specialized areas, and leaders in the Church Training program. In some churches the minister of adult education has the opportunity of working with an Adult Division director who is a volunteer working with the Sunday School. Each church, in counsel with the minister of education, must decide if this volunteer position is needed.

5. Relationships with Church Council Members

The church council is composed of the directors of the church program organizations, the chairman of the deacons, and various other leaders as designated by the church. As a member of the church council, the minister of adult education cooperates with this special group in planning, coordinating, and evaluating the adult work of the church. Annual calendar planning cuts down on static in the organizations and lowers the risk of poor relationships with staff and council members.

6. Relationships with Deacons

In some churches the minister of adult education, along with other staff members, is invited to be a part of the regular monthly meeting of the deacons. Each staff member has the opportunity of sharing his area of work with the deacons and asking for their questions and suggestions. This type of arrangement could increase positive relationships between staff and deacons.

7. Relationships with Church Committees

The minister of adult education usually works directly with some commitees. Sometimes these are special commitees assigned to him, and his advice and counsel are needed. During budget planning time he is expected to present his budget, through the proper channels, to the budget planning committee.

His expertise in programming enhances the balance of ministries because of the adults involved in all age groups. His role with the church nominating committee can be helpful to each staff member as he works closely to provide names of potential leaders for staffing all other groups. This assistance enhances relationships among committee and staff members.

The minister of adult education, working with other age-group workers, gives direction to the "Christian Service Survey" or talent survey that is taken in some churches. The information from this survey is turned over to the church nominating committee and can render a tremendous service in finding prospects for leadership positions in the church. (See the sample survey in this chapter.)

8. Relationships with Denominational Workers

Relationships with groups outside the church are important. It is good for the minister of adult education to have fellowship with other church staff members in the associations, including all denominations. There are some professional adult education organizations he may want to join. There are times when he should take his turn in serving in leadership positions in the association, in the state, and possibly in Southern Baptist Convention agencies.

As the minister of adult education does his work effectively by leading adults, he strengthens the work and relationships in the entire church. It is important that he perceive the importance of his role as it relates to each age-group worker. As each age-group worker leads out in the designated area, the educational program and the church will be strengthened and directed toward the ultimate objectives of the church: to worship, minister, educate, witness, and apply Bible truth.

The minister of adult education must depend on the leadership of the Holy Spirit and spend time in meditation, Bible study, and prayer if he is to have effective relationships with others.

VI. ACCEPT RESPONSIBILITY FOR SOME KEY LEADERSHIP ROLES

The minister of adult education is to the adult education program what the minister of education is to the total education program. Instead of working with all age groups, he strives to become a specialist, a professional in adult work. He is counselor, Bible leader, motivator, missions leader, minister. He works at the identity process in being knowledgeable in the areas of preschool, children, and youth work; but he directs most of his energies toward his adult role. His relationships and leadership role with the members of the church council, church program leaders, and other staff members have already been established in this chapter.

Recognizing, accepting, and working through the many roles of the minister of adult education mark the beginning of an effective ministry.

1. Plan, Promote, and Evaluate Adult Work

The minister of adult education plans individually and with all his workers. He recognizes his role in leading his workers to plan and to involve in the planning process persons with whom they work.

The minister of adult education should plan regularly with his Sunday School department directors. Many conduct this type of planning weekly, while some prefer monthly planning sessions. During the weekly fellowship meal the directors may eat together in a special area and be led in a planning session by the minister of adult education. This planning session would include helps for the regular weekly workers' meetings, a look at last Sunday (records, prospects, visitors, problem areas, and strong points), items of promotion (adult and churchwide), plans for the coming Sunday, and calendar dates. Many of the routine announcements may be included in the regular Wednesday newssheet, thus saving time in this planning session. As a follow-up to this meeting, the minister of adult education may include in the "Director's Notes" distributed to each adult department director on Sunday morning, items to be stressed in the Sunday department period.

Department periods and Bible study sessions should blend together. This accomplishment requires planning. It is done through the weekly department planning led by department directors and the teaching improvement period conducted by the department director or someone qualified to serve as teaching improvement leader.

The role of the minister of adult education is to see that the weekly workers' meeting is conducted by trained leaders who are committed to outreach and the task of better Bible teaching. "The purpose of adult Sunday School work is to help Christian and non-Christian adults, no matter what their stage of growth, to become more whole, complete, and perfect children of God. And they should be helped to become involved in the mission of Jesus Christ." [8] All plans for Sunday should be launched with this purpose in mind; the staff member should pray that God might use them to his glory.

The monthly publication *Adult Leadership* magazine has regular helps for planning and conducting the Sunday morning department period and the weekly workers' meeting. The minister of adult education sees that this periodical and other planning tools are available for the Adult workers.

A quarterly workshop for Adult department directors can be most beneficial in planning and evaluating adult work. The minister of adult education sets these dates after consultation with the directors. Each director is given opportunity to suggest items for the agenda. This meeting could be held in the home of one of the adult directors. It is a time of prayer, in-depth planning, looking to the future for leadership needs, reviewing vacancies, suggesting names of potential leaders for approval by the nominating committee, projecting calendar dates, discussing space and equipment needs, and evaluating past program activities.

The pastor, administrator, minister of education, and other age-group ministers may be invited to observe and share helpful suggestions from their special area. A minimum of two hours should be allotted for this meeting. A prepared agenda will help keep this planning session on target. The workshop can be concluded with light refreshments and a time of fellowship.

An annual retreat for all adult workers is another excellent planning opportunity. Conducted away from the church at a retreat area, lake, or country home of one of the members, the retreat can be fruitful in planning and in providing an excellent opportunity for Christian fellowship. Persons who work with adults in Sunday School, Church Training, and missions organizations should be included in the annual retreat.

Monthly or quarterly planning sessions with Church Training leaders are vital to a meaningful and continuous church training program. Ideas for curriculum materials, resource materials, and study leaders can be shared. Study groups can be projected in advance and adequate promotion given to each topic.

The minister of adult education also has opportunity to work with department and class leaders in planning retreats, seminars, weekday Bible study opportunities, the annual adult Vacation Bible School, and teacher appreciation day.

Observing Adult Day in the church gives the minister of adult education the opportunity for recognizing and expressing appreciation for all adult leaders, calling attention to achievements of adults and publicizing plans for future adult work. Some churches choose to spread the Adult emphasis throughout the year by recognizing special groups of adults such as singles, homebound, internationals, and senior adults. Sometimes the church may choose to tie in the young adult emphasis with the annual baby day. This day is a time when some churches recognize all new babies born during the previous year by having parental dedication in the morning worship service.

The minister of adult education works with adults and church leaders in designing appropriate publicity material for churchwide use and for use in the Adult Division.

Evaluating is a continuous process in the Adult Division. The minister of adult education will constantly be evaluating his work personally and each phase of the adult work in the church. When evaluation instruments are used, he should give careful attention to suggestions made. The fruitfulness of future surveys will hinge on effective follow-up of suggestions already given. The questionnaire in this chapter may serve as a guide.

ADULT QUESTIONNAIRE

Department_____Class_____

1. How do you feel about the length of time spent in the Sunday School department period?

Too short_____Too long_____About right_____

2. Is the content or program of the department period relevant and meaningful to you?

Yes_____No_____

3. Is the method of presentation by department leaders satisfactory to you?

Yes_____No_____

4. Do you favor serving coffee and doughnuts or other refreshments before the Sunday School class time?

Yes_____No_____

5. What specific suggestions can you offer that would make the department period more meaningful? (Use back of page if necessary.)

6. Is there adequate allowance for fellowship with others in your department, other than members of your class?
Yes_____No_____

7. Is there adequate time for the class sessions on Sunday mornings?
Yes_____No_____

8. Is there a wholesome sense of fellowship with the members of your class?
Yes_____No_____

9. Is the content of the material studied and discussed in the class relevant and meaningful to you?
Yes_____No_____

10. Is the teaching procedure in your class satisfactory to you?
Yes_____No_____

11. If you were to become teacher of your class, what changes would you like to make, beginning immediately?

12. Do you feel your class is organized to meet the needs of the members?
Yes_____No_____

13. If you were to drop out of Sunday School, what would be the principal reason?

14. Are you encouraged to use your Bible in the class sessions?
Yes_____No_____

Thank you for your help!

2. Give Assistance in Organizing and Training

The role of organizer is of tremendous importance as it relates to the minister of adult education. By working through the church nominating committee, he sees that each area of the adult work is staffed with qualified, dedicated, and trained leaders. He checks before they are enlisted to be sure that prospective leaders are committed to training, Bible study, prayer, planning sessions, outreach, regular attendance, and ministry.

The ministry of adult education will plan workshops for department leaders, class leaders, and teachers. Persons qualifying in each of these areas should be enlisted to lead the workshops. In order to assure availability of competent workshop leaders, invitations should be issued several months in advance. Associational training schools are planned in many associations early in the fall to help in training leaders. Special Sunday School and Church Training weeks during the summer at a state assembly or at one of the Convention-wide conference centers will be invaluable in training adult leaders for new positions of leadership. Reservations for Ridgecrest or Glorieta Conference Centers need to be made the last of December or in early January.

The minister of adult education consults with class teachers, outreach leaders, and group leaders to be sure they understand the "group plan of work" in the Adult class. By organizing with an effective group leader for every four to seven members, the class is prepared for outreach and ministry.

Keeping the Adult area organized throughout the year is a continuous job. The program must be balanced to meet the needs of all adults. New units should be added as needed. Adding new units means additional leaders, curriculum materials, extra training, and adequate space and equipment.

Church Training and the weekly workers' meetings serve as continuous training opportunities for all adult leaders. New member training, a vital part of Church Training, helps to introduce new adult church members to the church and the Adult Division. In working with the person elected to direct the new member program, the minister of adult education may share one of the sessions to introduce himself and to give an overview of the work in the Adult Division.

The minister of adult education should set the example by being well organized and by continuously updating his training skills. He should be a teacher of teachers, volunteering to lead the teaching improvement period regularly by previewing a new unit of study or by reviewing next Sunday's lesson with the Adult teachers.

3. Lead in a Program of Outreach

Outreach has always characterized successful churches. A program of outreach must be carefully planned. Of all the leadership roles, the minister of adult education may find this role to be the toughest.

Working through the department and class outreach leaders, he seeks to involve the class group leaders and members in a regular program of outreach. This means finding prospects, assigning them by age to departments and classes, encouraging regular visitation sessions, and following up on prospects that require cultivation in order to be reached. The minister of adult education, working through his leaders, uses the weekly workers' meeting to promote and plan the outreach program.

Successful outreach requires prospect analysis meetings. The minister of adult education involves other age-group workers in an evaluation of each prospect, seeking to find the key to reaching for Christ and the church not only the adults but also the family. Special visitation plans may be adopted to reach the homebound, the singles, and the special groups already mentioned in this chapter.

4. Promote Christian Fellowship

Fellowship is one ingredient missing in so many areas of adult work. Another role of the minister of adult education is to promote and plan for Christian fellowship. A party is *not* always a prerequisite for fellowship. With proper planning there can be a feeling of fellowship in a Sunday department period and the class session. The minister of adults, working through department and class leaders, can help improve the fellowship opportunities on Sunday morning by leading directors to use a variety of people in the department period and to recognize prospects and visitors. The outreach leaders need to be trained to be aware of new faces.

The class meeting, in addition to being a time of planning, Bible study, and encouragement in outreach activities, should also be a time of Christian fellowship.

There seems to have always been more feeling of fellowship in Church Training groups. The minister of adult education can use the Church Training hour to explore new ideas and to establish special seminars in needed areas such as divorce, death, dying, and aging.

Small groups may be organized to help members grow in self-awareness, interpersonal effectiveness, and their relationship to God. Discovery groups may be designed to encourage the process of discovering, interpreting, and putting into action spiritual gifts presented in the Bible.

All these ideas can be meaningful learning experiences that, in turn, produce a growing feeling of real fellowship in the church.

The minister of adults can lead the adults to plan after-church fellowships and a churchwide picnic in which *all* members of the family participate. He can work with the church recreation committee in planning recreation activities for special groups of adults and for all adults and their families.

Some ministers of adults have used the idea of "Four Fabulous Fellowship" to build fellowship among the church family. Sponsored by the Adult Division, this is a concerted effort to combine four couples together for fellowship over a four–month period. The purpose is to form associations among church members who may not know each other in the beginning but who will establish lasting friendships because of a planned fellowship together once each month for four months.

5. Lead and Train Adults in Ministry

One of the most rewarding roles of the minister of adult education is that of ministry, "meeting the crisis needs of others in the name of Christ." Leading and training adult members to engage in ministry activities, personally and through organized class and department efforts, is vital and is an activity that was the focal point in the teachings and ministry of Jesus.

The minister of adult education may assist in the worship service, preach on occasions, conduct funerals and weddings upon request, visit in the hospitals, minister to special needs, and serve as counselor.

The minister of adult education can become isolated with his "Adults only" role. However, he may choose to be an active participant in the church VBS, church camps, staff recreational activities, and missions projects, as appropriate.

VII. Possess Some Leadership Qualifications

1. A Call from God

The minister of adult education is a God-called minister. "He must have had an experience with God out of which has come his convictions that he is doing the work which God has for him to do." [9] It is this divine call that will see him through times of doubt and disappointment and will give new direction and strength to his life. He must have a growing and dynamic faith, resulting from a disciplined life of consistency in Bible study and prayer, if he is to be a spiritual leader. "Prayer, Bible study, devotional reading and meditation are still basic to Christian growth." [10]

He should constantly be concerned about leading men and women to a saving knowledge of Jesus Christ. He must lead the people with whom he works to share his evangelistic spirit.

2. Training

The minister of adult education should prepare himself educationally. Formal education including college and seminary training should be high on his list of priorities. A call to serve God is a call to prepare. It involves getting all the training possible to be prepared for God's calling. We need to be reminded that Christ spent thirty years preparing for his three-year ministry.

Training in administrative skills, a knowledge of the work of all church program organizations, and a clear understanding of the developmental tasks of each adult age group should be basic in the preparation for this position. Five to ten years of experience as a minister of education would further help train this person for the job. His ability to know the total work of all church organizations would give him invaluable insight into being objective in assisting in all adult-led areas of service. The use of internship is an excellent training opportunity.

There is a growing demand for ministers of adult education. There is a limited number of experienced people serving in this position in the local church. These facts mean that interested churches often must choose a recent graduate from the seminary. Adult education courses can provide the background and springboard for service.

3. Commitment to Learn

A minister of adult education must continue to learn if he remains effective. He must be consistent in his effort to remain creative and innovative. He must stay abreast of educational trends by consistently reading new books and professional journals related to his field and by studying new materials to determine their relevancy. Education is a lifelong process. Opportunities for new adventures in learning are offered by state, regional, Convention-wide, and national religious education associations. Southern Baptist seminaries, conference centers (Glorieta and Ridgecrest), and the Church Program Training Center at the Sunday School Board in Nashville, Tennessee, offer opportunities for continual learning.

A learner is not lazy. There is no substitute for hard work; hard work accounts for the success of most Adult programs in the church.

4. Resourcefulness

The minister of adult education should be the most resourceful person his adults know. He needs to keep up with new curriculum materials, study course books, leaflets, secular books in the adult field, resource kits, and workshops (association, state, Convention-wide, and secular).

Church Administration, Adult Leadership, and *Outreach* periodicals should be "required reading" each month. The minister of adult education needs to make sure that these items are ordered for him and his leaders from the Materials Services Department of the Sunday School Board in Nashville, Tennessee. Many other adult supplies are available from the Baptist Book Stores. The *Materials Services Catalog* is an invaluable tool for keeping up-to-date on materials.

The minister of adult education can keep up with change and learn new ideas by attending the annual meeting of all ministers of adult education. This group began meeting in 1975 and meets each year the latter part of November and the first few days of December. There are no elected officers, but one person is chosen to arrange the meeting. An agenda of topics for discussion is compiled by the group in its first session together. Each person attending is requested to bring a package of materials to share with the group.

5. Discipline

A disciplined life includes more than discipline in one's devotional and prayer life. Discipline in all areas of one's life is a leadership quality that should be developed by anyone responsible for training others.

A minister of adult education must spend time regularly listening to what the people are saying. This ability to listen creatively requires discipline.

In order to carry out the many facets of his work, the minister of adult education must learn to manage his time. Time management requires real discipline. A "do list" for each day is a good beginning toward managing one's time. Items on the list can be ranked in order of importance. This approach helps one to develop the habit of planning ahead and thinking through his work for the day. It will be surprising and rewarding to see how much more one accomplishes each day through this kind of planning.

6. Love for People

The success of the minister of adult education will depend on his genuine love for all people and his ability to work with them. "His own success and ability will be measured largely by his ability to get things done through other people." [11] He should be a friend of the persons with whom he works. He should be genuinely sincere and not seek to use people for his own personal gain.

One of the rewards of being a minister of adult education is having the opportunity to work closely with people and to see them grow and develop into mature Christians. He also may contribute significantly to helping equip them for their own ministry.

7. A Sense of Vision and Mission

Vision involves clarity and precision concerning objectives, purposes, and aims both for the minister of adults and the persons he seeks to lead. "Dr. John R. Mott has defined a man of vision as he who can see further than other men see, deeper than other men see, and before other men see." [12]

Decisiveness, under God's direction and leadership, is a kind of mental strength which every minister of adult education should develop. Vision without the ability of willingness to act upon it would accomplish little. Decisive leaders help to encourage decisiveness in others.

A minister of adult education should have his own personal objectives clearly in mind and be totally aware and committed to the ultimate mission of the church: "making God's love known to all men." This vision and understanding of mission will keep the work from becoming drudgery or routine. There will always be an excitement about the work as one sees people grow and develop, study God's word, and mature in their Christian experience.

The writer of this chapter expresses appreciation to the following ministers of adult education for their suggestions:

Dr. Bob Hines, South Main Baptist Church, Houston, Texas
Mr. Clois Smith, Tallowood Baptist Church, Houston, Texas

Mr. Jerry Spivey, Park Hill Baptist Church, North Little Rock, Arkansas.

Notes

1. Will Beal, comp., *The Work of the Minister of Education* (Nashville: Convention Press, 1976), pp. 15–16.

2. James D. Williams, *Guiding Adults* (Nashville: Convention Press, 1969), p. 4.

3. Roy B. Zuck and Gene A. Getz, eds., *Adult Education in the Church* (Chicago: Moody Press, 1970), p. 15.

4. Vernon R. Kraft, *The Director of Christian Education in the Local Church* (Chicago: Moody Press, 1957), p. 93.

5. Marvin T. Judy, *The Multiple Staff Ministry* (Nashville: Abingdon Press, 1969), p. 82.

6. Leonard E. Wedel, *Building and Maintaining a Church Staff* (Nashville: Broadman Press, 1966), p. 129.

7. Reginald M. McDonough, *Working with Volunteer Leaders in the Church* (Nashville: Broadman Press, 1976), p. 9.

8. Ernest Hollaway and James Fitch, comps., *Working with Adults in Sunday School* (Nashville: Convention Press, 1974), p. 5.

9. W. L. Howse, *The Church Staff and Its Work* (Nashville: Broadman Press, 1959), p. 102.

10. Robert E. Bingham and Ernest J. Loessner, *Serving with the Saints* (Nashville: Broadman Press, 1970), p. 95.

11. Joseph G. Mason, *How to Be a More Creative Executive* (New York: McGraw-Hill Co., Inc., 1960), p. 246.

12. Herman Harrell Horne, *The Essentials of Leadership* (Nashville: Cokesbury Press, 1931), p. 18.

CHRISTIAN SERVICE SURVEY

Name_____ Date_____
Residence_____ Phone_____
Business Address_____ Bus. Phone_____

AREAS OF RESPONSIBILITY	Church work you are now doing	Church work you have done before	Place you are willing to serve	If necessary for total program, would you accept change?
SUNDAY SCHOOL:				
General Officer (which?)				
Dept. Director				
Outreach Leader				
Group Leader				
Teacher (age group?)				
Cradle Roll Visitor				
Homebound Visitor (Extension)				
VBS (age group?)				
Other				
CHURCH TRAINING:				
General Officer (which?)				
Dept. Officer (which?)				
Leader or Sponsor (age?)				
Other				
WMU:				
General Officer (which?)				
Baptist Women				
Baptist Young Women				

Mission Friends Work				
G.A. Work				
Acteens Work				
Other				
BROTHERHOOD:				
General Officer (which?)				
R.A. Work				
Other				
GENERAL:				
Deacon				
Visit for Church				
Work on Committees (name)				
Food Service				
Recreation, Sports, etc.				
Typing, Office Work, Phoning				
Art Work (Posters, etc.)				
Teach in Nursery During Church				
Other				
MUSIC:				
Choir: Voice Part:				
Instrument Player				
Song Leader				
Help with Graded Choirs				
Other				

5.
The Minister of Youth Education

Tennyson said: "The old order changeth, yielding place to new; and God fulfills himself in many ways, lest one custom should corrupt the world." [1] When we realize that the very nature of the Christian faith includes change, we recognize that Jesus not only expected it but that he produced it. If the church is to be viewed as a living, changing organism rather than merely an institution, then we must discover the nature, purpose, and functions of the church as it relates to youth.

The first challenge a minister of youth education faces is the challenge of change as it relates to youth education.

I. DEVELOP A BASIC PHILOSOPHY OF YOUTH EDUCATION

Of all the areas relating to the ministry of religious education in local churches, perhaps there is less good, concrete, sound thinking concerning youth education. We desperately need a sound concept of what youth education is in a church.

Paradoxically, at the very time we are beginning to build for youth education a theological and educational foundation which has genuine promise, we are also experiencing something of a crisis in youth education. The church is being perceived as ineffective and "out of touch" by countless youth, both inside and outside the community of faith. Yet, matching the ones who are disenchanted, there are many who testify to having found significant growth in their church experiences. Thus any attempt to generalize about the relevance of the religious education of our youth will fail to find universal support when individual youth in varying churches are interviewed. Still, thoughtful leaders are deeply concerned about the growing numbers who are not responding to the traditional approaches to youth education.

The whole field of youth education seems to be in a state of flux. Old patterns are being abandoned, often not without resistance from parents and even youth for whom these approaches have had meaning. Feelings of guilt and gnawing defensiveness tend to confuse persons who are seeking seriously to reconstruct the church's ministry with youth. Such introspection and honest evaluation, however, have produced a period of solid theological reassessment concerning adequate goals, as well as creative experimentation in respect to curricula, settings, and methods for youth education.

Perhaps at no time in the history of Southern Baptists has there been a greater emphasis on youth in the churches. To the disdain of many, activities are on the throne instead of life-changing educational experiences. It is more than a battle of semantics. Lest you miss the emphasis of this writer, youth activities should be an outgrowth of youth education. It's not a matter of either/or, but of both/and.[2]

1. Understand That the Life Needs of Youth Are Complicated by Rapid Change

Inherent in a change of concept regarding youth education is also a recognition of the need to rethink the life needs of contemporary youth. No one would be foolish enough to express the idea that youth throughout the centuries have not had some basic needs. But against a backdrop of our culture, there are the peculiar needs of youth today.

Today's youth are maturing in a rapidly changing, complex society—a society whose future dimensions are shrouded in uncertainty and whose present hope for stability is often torn by disillusionment and doubt for the many and tragedy for the few.

A cluster of thoughts would indicate that the adolescent's devel-

opment is influenced by changes in such social institutions as the
family, the school, peer groups, the world of work, and the conflicts
that take place in all of these groups—his society. Family problems
in a nuclear age have increased drastically in the past few years.
In a day when many problems are more complex, political and
social activism has declined. Yet the so-called sexual revolution
and the loss of confidence in social institutions, including government, has continued. The affluent society of less than ten years,
with an overabundance of jobs, has been replaced by a society of
lowered expectations with historically high unemployment for
youth, especially minority youth. One of the most recent concerns
of the government has been to produce jobs for youth. With reduced budgets, social tensions, and renewed questioning of the
fundamental purposes of education, our culture has created a problem that the church cannot ignore in its ministry with youth.

The lowering of the mandatory age for attending public school
is a factor. In addition, some public-school administrators are con-
templating such things as a 45–15 attendance plan, which would
indicate that a student in the high school years would go to school
forty-five days and then would be off fifteen days over a period
of eleven months. This schedule alone, if it were to be adopted,
would have extreme repercussions for a church's programming
for youth education.

Changing sex roles, particularly for women, are causing not only
changing vocational and educational opportunities, but also are
effecting a reappraisal of personal goals. One national television
network produces a program in which the woman in the show
takes complete male habits or roles and the man takes the woman's
roles, a complete reversal of the traditional sex roles of the man
and woman. These changes cannot help but affect and influence
the life needs of youth. Other changes that are occurring include
patterns of drug use and alienation, as well as psychological problems of teenagers.

John Janeway Conger, a pediatrician with the University of Colo-
rado School of Medicine, has recently revised his book *Adolescence*

and Youth. Ironically, his first edition was published only four years previously. Already it is outdated. Conger insists that the reason for a new edition is because the psychological problems of adolescents have changed. An authority like Conger is certainly one of many who would shout volumes to the church to rethink the life needs of youth.

2. Recognize That Youth Life-Styles Are Psychologically Induced

The teen years or, as John Claypool calls them, "the walk through the valley of the shadow of adolescence," are like a person riding a horse backward through life. This trek is disconcerting and revolting to the teenager because he sees things almost after he passes through them. This perspective makes youth a reactionary time of life, a time of life that offers something painful for everybody— or, as Ed Seabough dubbed it, "the period of no more and not yet."

This walk through the "valley of the shadow of adolescence" has many stopovers. Some are peculiar to junior high youth, while others are distinctive experiences of the senior high youth. The adolescent must stop at the blooming of his body. When he experiences the growth spurt and the rapid, extraordinary physiological changes, certainly he needs assurance that reminds him of the beautiful old story "The Ugly Duckling." Again he experiences the epidemic of inferiority which is best expressed in that old folk tune, "Nobody loves me; everybody hates me; guess I'll go eat worms." This period of self-hate projects itself into hatred for other people. He sees himself as inadequate, inept. This epidemic needs to be met with the reassurance that "God don't make no junk."

A third stop of this trek is influenced by the cult of conformity. This cult pushes youth to follow the whims of the group. It is the herd instinct at work. The tyranny of pressure with regard to clothes and hair brings strain on the relationships between parents and youth as well as other adults.

Frightening to most adults and disconcerting to nearly every adolescent is the confrontation with the crack of confusion when the teenager is moving from what he has been told to what he is going to believe. With thoughts, opinions, and decisions making one's head swim, he moves out of idealism to realism while seeking to appropriate unto himself a personal value system. This system crystallizes from a cultural milieu of experiences, education, training, home, and institutions. Sound, systematic Bible study is needed as well as study in systematic theology and Christian ethics. A major challenge to the church's education program for youth is to help them appropriate unto themselves a personal faith and an experience with the Lord. God does not have any grand-children!

This walk toward a personal value system is syncopated by the elevator of emotions so typical of the teenager: higher than a kite one moment and lower than a gopher's hole the next! One day the teenagers are adults; the next day they are children. The irony of this is that oftimes they simply become what adults expect, right or wrong.

As if the trauma of the elevator of emotions is not sufficient, next the teenager is flooded by the spring of sexuality, which comes to every teenager as inevitably as the sunrise—not sex per se, but total personhood: what it means to be a male or a female. This spring of sexuality is closely related to the teenager's self-concept. The link between irresponsible sex activity and low self-image is frightening.

No sooner do youth experience this spring than they are engulfed with the episode of emancipation from a dependency role. Actually they should be guided to move not from dependency to independence but to interdependence. This task suggests that the teenager learn to pick up what is being laid down and walk forward without walking away from his sources, stretching and expanding a relationship so that everything becomes bigger without snapping or exploding the bond. Is not this trek sufficient challenge for the church to rethink the life needs of youth?

3. Accept the Challenge That Youth Education Deserves Fresh Insights

There are some misunderstandings concerning youth education in the church that need to be exposed to intelligent thinking rather than darkened by prejudiced presuppositions. Some time ago Bob Taylor of the Sunday School Board and I shared similar feelings that were later entitled "Myths of Youth Ministries." They provide insights needed in developing an acceptable statement of philosophy of youth education.

Myth 1:—Recreation is the primary function of the minister of youth education. It is ironic that while some churches try to make youth programs all serious, there are still churches who try to make it all fun. It is the wise church that strives for a balance between the fun and the faith-learning experiences. This myth manifests itself in a baby-sitting service for youth; it is a carry-over from an inadequate concept of children's activities. Recreational events such as retreats, fellowships, and parties are valid; but they are to be viewed as an outgrowth of youth education, not the sum total. Youth education is the fuel that keeps the flame burning; activities provide the warmth that one feels as a result. Certainly recreation is a part of those activities that promote the growth of a Christian youth in knowledge, appreciations, and skills for Christian discipleship; but it is by no means the totality of youth's needs in the teen years.

Myth 2:—The minister of youth education must be a young person. Over the last four years I have surveyed many audiences, asking them two questions: (1) What is the name of the person (other than parents) who made the greatest contribution to your life when you were a teenager? (2) What was the age of that person when he made that contribution to your life?

Almost without exception the response has been a teacher, a pastor, a minister of music, a coach or Scout leader, a next-door-neighbor, or an employer well over the age of thirty. Against this background is the paradox of the church employing a young youth minister with the intention of his giving "a shot in the arm" with a Pied-Piper approach to youth programs. If this myth can be exploded, some significant problems in youth programs can be overcome. Age is not a primary factor in who can effectively lead youth. A more mature person may be willing to go to a church and stay long enough to make a contribution to the church and the youth.

Myth 3:—The minister of youth education should be a person with charisma. Far too many of our churches and potential youth leaders (as well as parents) feel that to be an effective minister of youth, one must be a magnetic leader with the personality of the world's leading salesman, the talent of the world's greatest professional athlete, and the looks of a Greek god or goddess! Interestingly enough, some of the most unassuming, quiet, and average individuals have made indelible contributions on the lives of teenagers as youth ministers without being carnival hawkers.

Myth 4:—Youth education is exclusively a ministry with youth. Not so! Youth education calls for people who can challenge parents as well as youth. Due to the complexity of parenting today and the challenges that the family faces in rearing teenagers, the minister of youth education must develop a ministry with parents and the adults who work with youth. The need is to involve more adult leadership with youth rather than fewer. Parents everywhere long for assistance and support in parenting responsibilities.

Myth 5:—Youth education is a man's world. Certainly God is calling young men to serve in youth work, but he is also calling young women! Many youth have been touched by the lives of dedicated Christian women. It is unfortunate that there are many churches today who will not consider employing a woman as a minister of youth education. Overreaction to the women's liberation movement, thereby negating the possibility of women in youth work, is a mistake.

II. Build the Youth Education Program on Some Basic Concepts

Recognizing that a church may be guilty of becoming satisfied in the area of education, the minister of youth education needs a framework of basic principles for the youth education program. The tendency is that when programs develop, satisfaction sets in and the motivation becomes nothing more than perpetuating the status quo. The need then is to deorganize, not disorganize, and to let mobility and flexibility become the modus operandi. Stability is not a characteristic of the age, and affirming the biblical concept of ministry demands a program with youth which majors on education.

1. Some Givens Provide the Basic Framework for Youth Education

There are some givens in the church's ministry with youth. The first given is the gospel; the second, the world; the third, the person. The gospel is that which God has revealed to us which we affirm and experience as well as witness. The world is the existential situation. The person is the changing, maturing youth.

2. A Valid Objective Is Essential to Youth Education

These givens—the gospel, the world, and the person—produce a need for a new theological focus or objective for youth education. Divorcing the objective of religious education for youth from the objective of the total church is not the intention; rather, the purpose is to magnify the ministry to the youth culture.

An oft-quoted objective for religious education is that all persons be aware of God through his self-disclosure, especially his redeeming love as revealed in Jesus Christ, and that they respond in faith and love to the end that they may know who they are and what their human situation means, grow as sons of God in every relationship, fulfill their common discipleship in the world, and abide in Christian hope.[3]

In other words, the gospel is at the heart of our religious education, including youth education. The goal of the work with youth is to nurture them in the Christian community so that they will hear the gospel, experience its meaning, become aware of God's love in their lives, and respond in faith and love. This objective is to be reached by helping youth explore, in the light of the gospel, the field of Christian relationships that they are experiencing as adolescents and to discover, appropriate, and assume their responsibilities as Christians in their world. Youth need to be nurtured in the faith of their parents, but they also need a climate in which they may test this faith, refine it, and relate it to all their wider experiences so it can become their own firsthand faith.

3. Some Basic Characteristics Are Foundational in Youth Education

Certain characteristics must be considered foundational if youth education is to accomplish its objective.

Youth education is comprehensive in nature. It involves Sunday School, Church Training, music, and recreation. It is more than mission action, more than mission study. Youth education is all of these and more. The worship services, the prayer meetings, the visitation program, the churchwide evangelistic and outreach thrusts, the emphases on vocational guidance, family ministry, and personal counseling should all be seen as part of the youth education program of a church.

Youth education is a part of the total youth ministry. To speak of a youth ministry program is misleading. Such a statement falsely implies that the ministry of the church with youth is some separate entity.

In like fashion, to speak of the youth *ministries* of a church is inaccurate. *Programs* refer to Sunday School, Church Training, Acteens, Pioneers, and the youth choir. Thus a church has many youth programs, yet only one ministry with youth. Such a phrase seems to place the youth ministry outside a church's total, overarching, comprehensive ministry. In short, the phrase *youth ministries* confuses the total with the parts, the whole with the individual pieces.

A youth minister should see both the parts and the whole. He must see the total. His relationship to the total youth ministry will be stronger if he understands that he is to coordinate the total youth ministry. He is slighting his role as minister if he chooses to exert his leadership influence in some areas at the expense of other areas. Of course, there are priorities. It is true that all programs are not of equal importance. However, the singular thrust of youth ministry must be emphasized.

Youth education is an evangelistic ministry. In John 10:10 Jesus said, "I am come that they might have life, and . . . have it more abundantly." Youth education is an abundant, life-giving ministry.

In Luke 19:10 Jesus said, "For the Son of man is come to seek and to save that which was lost." This same objective should characterize the youth education program of a church. A church should have as its major goal that of reaching youth who are lost—lost spiritually, lost emotionally, and lost socially.

The minister of youth education should see his role and the role of youth leaders as presenting clearly to youth the claims of the gospel, allowing youth to consider them carefully, and leading them to make a personal commitment to the truths of the gospel. To build solely on the needs and interests of the youth already in the church fellowship is to fail the youth who are yet to be reached.

Youth education is a teaching ministry. The Christian pilgrimage begins with a birth experience. Years and years of growing and maturing follow the experience of accepting Jesus Christ as Lord and Savior. Conversion is three-dimensional: an experience, a process, and a consummation.

The youth education program should provide a climate in which a Christian youth can and will grow spiritually as gifts are affirmed, as questions are answered, and as needs for involvement and acceptance are met.

Youth's need for growth experiences is met in many ways throughout a church's youth ministry, but nowhere is it met as uniquely and as adequately as through the main-line, ongoing, educational organizations. Through adequate curriculum materials, small-group learning experiences, individual attention, and personal involvement in learning sessions, these ongoing organizations are the bases for a successful, vibrant youth ministry. Sprinkled throughout these ongoing program activities are generous portions of fellowships, retreats, dramas, camps, and similar activities.

Youth education is a church ministry. Ephesians 5:25 states, "Christ also loved the church, and gave himself for it." Over and over again the Bible reinforces the fact that Jesus and his disciples loved the church. Although the Bible refers to the church as a universal body, it most often refers to it as a fellowship, a union of believers, a ministry. It never refers to the church as a building. The Bible supports the idea of the church being both scattered and gathered.

The church is clearly identified as an instrument of God. All references to it are positive and affirming. Because Jesus loved the church and because the Bible is so clear in its support of the church, a minister of youth education should share his love and this support. He should see that activities, projects, study emphases, and other such events build the church, not demean it or even neutralize it.

Youth education is a Bible-based ministry. Applying such biblical concepts as the dignity and worth of man, the centrality of the gospel, and the importance of the church will build the youth education program on a Bible base.

Furthermore, Bible study (Sunday School) should be magnified and firmly established as the basis program of work for youth. Out of this Bible study foundation grows the training program (Church Training), the missions program (Pioneers and Acteens), the music program, the recreation program, and the various emphases for youth in a church.

Youth education is a ministry of widely distributed leadership. The depth and the future strength of a youth ministry are generally in direct proportion to the number of people (adults and youth) who are involved in planning, promoting, and conducting youth education activities.

Youth education is a personal ministry. A minister of youth education works with groups, crowds, and numbers. But the youth minister must not lose interest in or concern for the individual. Like anyone else, youth must feel a personal concern from church leaders (including professional staff and volunteer workers); else they will either drop out altogether or move to the fringe of involvement.

III. DEFINE THE SCOPE OF THE RELIGIOUS EDUCATION PROGRAM FOR YOUTH

As already indicated, youth education is a very large and complex ministry. The minister of youth education needs to define fully the total scope of both the work and his approach to the task.

1. Work for a Balanced Program

Among the first things the minister of youth education must do is to organize and give direction to a well-balanced program of religious education for the youth constituency of the church. This program will include the activities provided through the ongoing organizations plus extra activities to help youth solve their problems and grow into capable Christian witnesses.

2. Develop an Integrated Program

The youth minister must recognize that the youth education program is a part of the educational mission of the entire church and that it is to be closely integrated with the overall objectives of the church. It is essential that he have genuine appreciation of and understanding for each phase of the church program, not seek to build his own kingdom.

3. Plan Programs with the Youth and Their Leaders

The planning responsibility has a twin: sharing of responsibility. Youth must share in the responsibility to the church. It is a ministry with them as they share with adults, both the staff and the lay leadership, in planning and promoting activities for the church. The guidance concept of leadership expresses confidence in the abilities of youth and allows them the freedom to fail—remembering that before one walks, he crawls.

4. Enlist Adequate Leadership for Youth

Tantamount to planning is leadership development and enlistment. This challenge recognizes that to neglect leadership is to neglect the life of the church, especially the education program. When one is securing workers for the task, the beginning point is with the realization that the key to divine action is human instruments. There must be pulpit emphases by the pastor to support the enlistment of workers; but when it comes to the task of enlisting, that must be done with vitality as well as efficiency. An enlistment procedure would include the following: Magnify the enlistment interview. Have the interview at the church. Show the potential youth worker the challenge and the opportunity as the duties are spelled out. Expose him to all curriculum resources. Ask him to pray about the invitation, and agree on a date for his decision.

5. Use Curriculum Materials Wisely

Caution should be used if the temptation is expressed to throw out the curriculum and study what interests the youth. Professionally designed curriculum is an educational architecture. It is an arrangement of materials and experiences to accomplish a specific purpose. The comprehensive and balanced curriculum prepared for youth in Southern Baptist churches will save the minister of youth education from that last desperate preparation or search for "something to use." More importantly, it will ensure that youth obtain a properly proportioned view of the Christian faith and not leave them to the mercy of strong personalities or the preferences and whims of a leader. Research indicates that a significant lack of depth and a generally confused attitude regarding doctrinal convictions in most youth have grown out of a piecemeal, kaleidoscope approach to curriculum.

IV. Make Youth Education a Team Effort

All ministers of youth education find themselves in a team relationship both as staff members and leaders of volunteer workers. Several guidelines will enhance the team effort.

1. Recognize the Pioneer Aspect of Multiple Staff Leadership

The multiple-staff ministry is a highly complex phenomenon. Although it has had forerunners throughout Christian history, it is in its present form new.

In churches with multiple staff, each staff member has both specific and general responsibilities contributing to the total ministry of the church. Each is called of God, entrusted with the gospel, and in most instances trained professionally. Each should invest himself completely in his own area of work and also help his colleagues in their work so that together the ministerial team advances the work of Christ in the lives of people.

2. Work Diligently at Staff Relationships

Good staff relationships grow out of the feeling that the relationship is permanent and is based on a common objective. A beginning step in good relationships is a wholesome acceptance of the pastor as the first among equals and the primary leader.

Good staff relationships are never forced; they are the result of compatibility involving mutual respect for one another. Secondary considerations include clear understandings of job descriptions, organizational structures, and lines of authority.

The maintaining of good interpersonal relationships within a staff comes about when staff members become the best friends of the church and seek to harmonize their differences on all issues. Planning the work together helps to prevent misunderstandings and strife. Certainly no staff member would encourage the criticism of any other staff member. Building into their schedules occasional periods of fellowship and recreation cultivates spiritual relationships as well as the human dimension of friendship.

3. Cultivate Parent/Leader Relationships

The developing of treasured relationships in the ministry of youth includes the developing of good parental relations. Because youth live in families and these families form the circumstances in which the youth are developing as disciples, the minister of youth education must take advantage of opportunities to know and minister to parents of youth.

Be available for counseling in family problems and handling of communications with teenagers.

Provide activities for youth in which parents can find pride and joy in their children.

Use the parents' expertise in the program of the church. Parents provide a wealth of special training and talent that can be harnessed.

Provide activities for parents and youth to be together.

Visit in the home of the parents—not just for the teenager, but also for the parents.

Correspond with the parents periodically, keeping them abreast of the activities and programs.

Use the parents as counselors on retreats, choir trips, and the like, in addition to involving them in ongoing leadership responsibilities.

Encourage Sunday School teachers and Church Training workers in the Youth Division to visit the homes at strategic times to help parents with their children.

Ask the advice of parents about what their children need—or, better still, what they want their church to do for their teenagers.

Establish a resource center of books, pamphlets, and other materials for use by parents and youth interested in parent-teen relationships.

4. Keep the Relationships with Youth Wholesome

Finally, the quality of the relationships of the minister of youth education is firmly planted in his relationships with the youth. What do youth look for? It would be possible to print page upon page of qualities and traits deemed necessary and valuable for a minister of youth education. Inherent in the personality of the competent minister to youth is an authentic, genuine faith that always reflects itself against the built-in "bunk" detector which teenagers possess. Good relationships with teenagers spring from a basic incorruptible integrity, balanced with a sense of love and trust for youth, surrounded with an abundant energy and enthusiasm for the task, coated with communication skills, redeemed by a saving sense of humor, and topped off with a ministry to youth as a lifelong commitment.

V. KEEP THE SPIRITUAL PERSPECTIVE FOREMOST

If we are to attract and hold youth, leaders must rediscover and make manifest the power and the spirit of God not only through personal encounter, but also by helping youth to have such an encounter.

Notes

1. Alfred, Lord Tennyson, *The Passing of Arthur.*
2. Philip H. Briggs, "Youth Activities versus Education," *Search,* January 1977.
3. "We Have This Ministry" 2 (New York: National Council of Churches, 1964), p. 12.

6.
The Minister of Childhood Education

The religious education of children has played an important role in both Jewish tradition and the Christian context. Recognition of the need for the religious education of children is all but instinctive for parents, and its significance is amply portrayed in both the Bible and human experience.

Because of these facts it seems unnecesary to make a case for the religious education of children. A simple but comprehensive statement of philosophy should be sufficient. For the purpose of this book the following statement seems adequate. Christianity has an all-important message that is worth passing on to future generations. Inherent in Christianity is the obligation to pass it on in ways that can be understood by children.

The children's program of religious education in Southern Baptist churches consists of four interrelated but distinctive structures. They are Bible Teaching, Church Training, missions education, and music activities.

An increasing number of churches are providing a staff member to lead the religious education experiences of children. In this role the minister of childhood education is responsible for planning, coordinating, and/or directing the best possible educational experiences for the children of the church and for children who are prospects. The remainder of this chapter is dedicated to making this ministry as effective as any other in the church.

I. QUALIFY FOR THE POSITION

Every person who serves on a church staff must have some personal qualifications.

1. Be Called to the Work

Growing out of one's experience of salvation is a conviction that he is called to serve God. The minister of childhood education cannot be an exception to this rule. He must be sure that childhood education is the special area of work that God has assigned. In this assurance is the strength of one's leadership because he knows that he is in the center of God's will.

2. Know Basic Childhood Psychology

Educational work is essentially the guidance of the growth and development of persons. The obvious implication is that the leader of children's work in a church must know and be able to communicate characteristics, developmental stages, and needs of children.

3. Have the Essential Personal Qualities

Working with children and leaders in childhood education requires a growing love and appreciation for children. It also calls for an abundant supply of patience, wise judgment, tact, self-control, faith, cooperativeness, and good humor. All of these personal qualities will need to be bathed in prayer for the children, fellow workers, and parents.

4. Secure Training and Experience

The ideal goal for the minister of childhood education is to earn a degree in elementary education and to do graduate work in childhood education at a Southern Baptist seminary. Coupled with this academic preparation is the need for broad experience in a church. It is very difficult for a person who has little or no training and experience to make the decisions, train the workers, and do the necessary planning required in this position.

Although a formal education best prepares a person for childhood education, some capable persons have come to be real experts in the field by diligent work and self-teaching. Nevertheless, there seems to be no alternative to a measure of successful experience prior to becoming a staff member.

Continuing self-education is essential to the success of every minister of childhood education. The conscientious church staff member will read everything possible relating to children, including professional books and publications in his field. He will not assume that his education is complete with the end of formal training, but he will continue all his life to equip himself more fully for his great task.

5. Develop Skills in Working with Adults

The minister of childhood education needs to be aware that most of his work will be with adults, leading them to know how to work with childen. He must be thoroughly capable of teaching children himself in order to train others, but he must be equally skilled in teaching, leading, and motivating adults. These skills can be acquired through reading books on the subject, attending workshops, and through practice.

The last word has not been written about education and learning. The religious educator is obligated to adopt any new and better approaches to teaching/learning and religious education, as well as to stay open to new ideas that are *better* ideas.

II. Understand the Essential Relationships

Because church fields, needs, job requirements, and scope of responsibilities vary greatly, it is most difficult to propose an organization chart that is useful in and acceptable to every church. However, a good organization chart is helpful in determining the many relationships and interrelationships involved in the assignment as minister of childhood education. The chart in this chapter is a good beginning place for the church that needs to develop or reconsider its organizational relationships.

The minister of childhood education has horizontal and vertical program relationships as well as administrative relationships. He relates vertically to the minister of education and ultimately to the pastor. If there are multiple departments in the Children's Division, he relates also to the division director(s) responsible for Sunday School and/or Church Training departments. (The term "division director" generally refers to a lay leader who works only with one program organization. "Coordinator" designates a lay leader who works with more than one program organization in a church.)

The horizontal relationships are with the Girls in Action director, the Crusader RA leader, and the person responsible for the children's music program. The music leader may be a children's music division director or a minister of music. Horizontal relationships with the GA director, Crusader RA leader, and the children's music division director are correlating relationships. The minister of childhood education should offer assistance to the director, leader, and division director in securing workers in the organizations; assist in training these workers in child development and teaching methods; work with their leaders in determining meeting rooms; and be responsible for calendaring children's activities in each organization so as not to have overlapping.

Because it is difficult for any leader to supervise the work of more than eight persons, the minister of childhood education will almost always need to use division directors or coordinators if his administration is to be fully effective. This approach to getting the work done makes it imperative that the minister of childhood education stay abreast of new discoveries in teaching/learning for his age group and continue to equip himself and co-workers for his ministry.

Every church staff position requires a leader who is able to cooperate fully as a team member. The minister of childhood education, like other staff members, should earn the right to be an authority in his area of work. When this recognition has been established, he should be heard and his convictions should be given full consideration in decisions that relate to his responsibilities. Otherwise it is unfair to hold staff responsible for the outcome of the decision. A pastor and staff who accept each other as knowledgeable and competent in their respective specialties will have little difficulty in maintaining a wholesome Christian attitude and supportive working relationship.

III. Handle the Whole Range of Responsibility

The specific responsibilities of the minister of childhood education are generally determined by the job description adopted by the church. However, these duties are almost as varied as the churches that develop the requirements. Most churches expect their minister of childhood education to work in the following areas:

1. Establish Objectives and Goals for Children's Workers and Programs

The minister responsible for children's work should base all plans for the year on objectives and goals set by the church. He will meet with coordinators, division directors, and department leaders to share long-range plans of the church and to guide in setting objectives and goals for the Children's Division.

2. Plan and Submit Budget for Children's Division

A budget for childhood education will vary greatly from church to church, depending on the extent of the program. The minister of childhood education will prepare and submit his budget in the form used by his church. It would include major program expenses, which are broken down into such specifics as children's day camp, resident camp, Vacation Bible School, expendable supplies, social activities, children's night, stay-for-church clubs, parent meetings, or any unusual program item being planned.

The budget would probably also include literature for children and workers for the year. In some churches the minister of childhood education is responsible for budgeting for literature for all children's organizations; in some he budgets only for Sunday School and Church Training.

Crusader RA and Girls in Action program budgets are usually included in many Children's Division budgets.

Sometimes Vacation Bible School budgets are listed for all age levels in an education ministry category. Whenever it is thus listed, an estimate of expense in the Children's Division must be pepared and submitted.

An important item to be included in a budget request is an amount for staff improvement. This would include expenses to the conference centers, conventions, seminars, workshops, and other meetings which the minister of childhood education needs to attend. These and other budget items are proposed on the basis of the previous year's expenses, plus or minus projected programs for the new year.

3. Assist Division Directors or Coordinators in Enlisting and Evaluating Workers

When there are multiple departments for each age or grade and division directors or coordinators are used, the minister of childhood education will meet regularly with these leaders to discuss worker needs and possible workers and to offer suggestions.

The minister of childhood education will maintain a file of prospective workers for his division. Names may be secured from many sources. One good source is a talent sheet filled out by new members of the church. However, it is a good practice generally to delay asking new church members to work for about six months to a year, or according to the church policy. This delay allows new members time to meet and make friends of their own age. It also allows a minister of childhood education time to evaluate more accurately the leadership potential of new members.

Another reliable source of workers is parents of the children themselves. In visiting their homes the staff member can recognize the respect or lack of it a parent has for his own child. Also, a well-adjusted child usually has parents who are largely responsible for his good adjustment and would probably make a similar contribution to other childen.

New Vacation Bible School workers are an excellent source of potential teachers. Names of persons could be added to the list of prospective workers and contacted as needed.

It is hoped that the staff member responsible for children would never feel the need to ask for volunteers to teach children. He should be selective. If he asks for a volunteer he is in effect saying, "Just *anybody* will do; I am desperate!" And just *anybody* will not do to teach children. God calls people to teach each age group, and it is the God-called person that the minister of childhood education seeks. He will not be satisfied with someone who will merely tolerate children, use the teaching position to feed his own ego, or take a position simply to avoid being in an Adult Sunday School class.

Particular skills are needed to teach childen. Persons having these skills or who are willing to train to acquire these skills are the ones to be used.

Worker evaluation may be done at the regular meetings with coordinators or division directors. Every church staff member has a worker or two who could improve or who perhaps should be replaced. But if the minister of childhood education will remember that he is not only responsible for the children in his division but also for the nurture, training, and growth of the workers, he will do all in his power to help that worker grow spiritually and improve in needed skills.

It is a rare thing that a worker is so out of place in the Children's Division that he is totally unhappy. But if this situation should occur, the minister of childhood education will work with other age-level staff in offering this worker a responsibility in another area.

A situation could possibly arise in which the minister of childhood education felt he must ask for the resignation of a teacher. This action would be considered a very last resort and would be done only after much prayer, offering a change of responsibility, providing additional training, and consulting with the minister of education and perhaps the pastor also. Then the minister of childhood education would have a private conference with the offending teacher and in love explain how he feels this teacher would perhaps enjoy a change of responsibility.

Most churches resolve the problem of the unequipped teacher by enlisting teachers for one year only. The teacher would be aware of this policy and know that at the end of the year he would have an evaluation meeting with the minister of childhood education to determine whether he continued to teach. Of course, this approach would not be used until it was a policy throughout the church and fully understood and approved by the people.

4. Develop and Implement a Training Program for Workers

Convention-wide, statewide, and association-wide training events should be placed on the church calendar first and other training events planned to supplement. Though more workers are perhaps enlisted prior to promotion day than any other time, additional workers are needed from time to time throughout the year. To meet this need, the minister of childhood education will work with other age-level staff in planning churchwide training seminars, in addition to the Convention, state, and associational training events.

There should be at least one training conference in a church during the year to focus on children and how they learn. This conference would be promoted for all workers with children in all programs. In addition, the minister of childhood education would work with the GA director, RA leader, children's music division director, and Sunday School and Church Training division directors or coordinators to plan specific training conferences for each program.

Ongoing training is also needed. The special training events are excellent, but all workers may not be able to attend. Individual study or workshops during regular workers' planning meetings may be the only way some people can train. The minister of childhood education should work toward establishing a learning center for children's workers. The center could be set up in any available room in the church. It would contain all Children's Division study course books for each organization, all filmstrips, and the *Teacher Competency Kits* provided by Southern Baptist agencies. Often excellent materials on child development are available through public schools and libraries.

Filmstrip viewers and cassette players for individual or small group use would be provided. The learning center could be kept open for teachers, prospective teachers, or even parents on Sunday night, Wednesday night, and any other times needed. The minister of childhood education would set the room up and keep materials updated, but perhaps would need to enlist a training director or persons to remain in the center while it is open to assist workers and prospective workers with materials and equipment.

5. Plan for and Provide Adequate Space and Furnishings

Almost every Baptist church has a building and planning committee that would be instrumental in building new buildings or remodeling present space. The minister of childhood education will serve as a consultant and advisor to this committee when new or remodeled space is a possibility. He will work closely with the architect for such a facility, offering a list of requirements for his area and approving plans before they are finalized.

The minister of childhood education would serve in the same capacity for the committee responsible for purchasing furnishings for children's departments.

This approach presupposes that the minister of childhood education is thoroughly knowledgeable in these areas, keeps abreast of better equipment and furnishings available for the Children's Division, and works within the budget available to him for this purpose.

The minister of childhood education will consult with the GA director, RA leader, children's music division director, and Sunday School and Church Training division directors or coordinators to ensure that their needs will be met in the rooms which all program organizations will use.

6. Order Literature for the Children's Program Organizations

Literature needs are determined by the number of children and workers enrolled, plus projected enrollment increases. The budget allowance for literature will also be considered. The minister of childhood education usually orders the Sunday School and Church Training literature from The Baptist Sunday School Board. In some churches the WMU director or WMU secretary orders GA literature, and the Brotherhood director orders Crusader RA literature. The minister of childhood education offers assistance in those areas as needed. He would order pieces of all literature for himself and read through each piece. One reason for this is to acquaint himself with all units being studied so he will be able to offer suggestions for coordinating resources that can enrich the study for the children.

7. Secure Expendable Supplies and Other Resources for All Children's Organizations

Teaching is no better than the resources used. If good resources are readily available, they are much more likely to be used.

The rooms and supplies in the Children's Division at the church belong to the children using those rooms. They are provided by the church; they do not belong to individual teachers or even programs. A goal for the minister of childhood education is to promote this attitude if it does not already exist.

A children's resource center may be established in some unused room at the church. The minister of childhood education may purchase at wholesale prices all expendable supplies and keep this room stocked. As materials are used in department rooms by any organization for children, they could be replaced by items from the resource center.

A resource center director should be enlisted to be in this room to assist workers on Sunday morning and evening and Wednesday evening. He would be responsible for keeping the room in order so the materials could be more easily found and for keeping the minister of childhood education informed as to supplies needed.

8. Plan and Direct Vacation Bible School for Children

The minister of childhood education would calendar Vacation Bible School associational training conferences as well as church planning meetings and would seek to have Vacation Bible School directors enlisted early in the year. If division directors are used in Sunday School, they can be responsible for enlisting Vacation Bible School directors and for offering suggestions to the directors for workers in their departments.

The minister of childhood education would order Vacation Bible School literature in January and have it available for Vacation Bible School directors to give to their teachers as they are enlisted.

The minister of childhood education will meet with Vacation Bible School directors as soon as they are enlisted, perhaps in February. He will work with the directors and division directors to make decisions as to time of day of Vacation Bible School, whether to provide a noon meal for workers and their children, recreation schedules, refreshment procedures, joint worship service plans, and open house or parent night plans. All planning should be coordinated with the total Vacation Bible School program of activities. The minister of childhood education may want to print a VBS workers' handbook containing these plans, plus training and planning dates, and procedures for purchasing supplies—and to have it available for the workers as they are enlisted.

Following VBS the staff member for children will direct follow-up procedures with prospects for all organizations and with the pastor on any professions of faith made. He will also ensure that the Vacation Bible School reports are compiled and sent to the proper people.

9. Plan and/or Direct Day Camp

Either five consecutive days of day camp or one-day-a-week day camp for the summer is a great addition to a church's program for children.

If churchwide visitation is promoted one day a week, a day camp for elementary school age children could be a big asset to the visitation program. If the church has a Mother's Day Out one day a week, a summer day camp on that day would be a great help to mothers of preschoolers and school-age children. But the program is not just to give mothers a "day out"; it is a fun time and a teaching time for children. The minister of childhood education will want to carefully evaluate the teaching material to be used in day camp. Excellent day camping units are available through the missions organizations; they may be purchased at Baptist Book Stores.

A church may employ a summer assistant to direct day camps, using older high school and college students as counselors. Also, there are some parents who are able to serve in this capacity. If this help is volunteer, the cost to children can be minimal. If this help is paid, the cost per child will be set accordingly. Thorough training is an imperative for day camping counselors.

10. Plan and/or Direct Retreats for Older Childen

Fifth- and sixth-graders enjoy overnight retreats. Retreats can be spiritual "highs" for children at much-needed times. A back-to-school retreat in late summer can meet very real needs in children as they look forward to a new school year.

These plans would be made to meet specific needs in a local church. Sometimes fifth- and sixth-graders enjoy a Vacation Bible School retreat rather than regular Vacation Bible School.

11. Plan and Direct Children's Resident Camp

If a five-day resident camp is a possibility for older children in a church, it can be a highlight of the year. The minister of childhood education would plan and direct this camp as a revival for children, including Bible study, mission study, preaching (by the pastor if possible), recreation, and crafts. A successful children's camp will depend on an adequate number of well-trained counselors. A minimum number would be one counselor for every ten children, with a better ratio being one to every five to seven children.

12. Coordinate Division-wide Children's Parties

Department directors will want to plan at least quarterly socials for the children, with the teachers of some groups planning even more get-togethers. But there will be times during the year that coordinated parties would be to the advantage of the children and their parents. If all department Christmas parties could be planned for the same date and hour, better attendance could probably be had as well as easier calendaring for the church at busy times.

Other times might be Valentine Day, end-of-school parties, back-to-school parties, Thanksgiving parties, and the like.

13. Plan for Children During Churchwide Events

There are usually several times during a year when children will be at the church with parents, but will not necessarily be with their parents at the meetings. These could be events like stewardship banquets, Weeks of Prayer, teacher-training times, and home and family life workshops. The minister of childhood education would want to plan for these times, enlist and train volunteer workers to teach children, and make them the most meaningful sessions possible for the children.

14. Coordinate Publicity Through Various Church Media

The minister of childhood education would want to ensure good publicity for each children's program activity by preparing articles and announcements for the church paper, using displays on bulletin boards, planning mailouts, or making use of any other appropriate means of communication.

15. Plan for and Implement an Ongoing Visitation and Outreach Program

The staff member responsible for children will cooperate with the church program of visitation and promote such plans through division directors or coordinators. The very title of minister implies more than just outreach visitation. The staff member seeks to minister to children, their teachers, and their families. He will also accept other visitation assignments, such as hospital visitation, as shared by administrative staff members.

16. Coordinate Plans for Parent Meetings

There are parenting needs that could be met in parent meetings which are supported by all children's program organizations. At the same time there are parent meetings that would specifically apply to one organization, such as one to explain the objectives of the organization or to enlist cooperation of parents in home study with children to correlate with work done at church. The minister of childhood education can coordinate these activities in order to avoid overlapping and to better meet parents' needs.

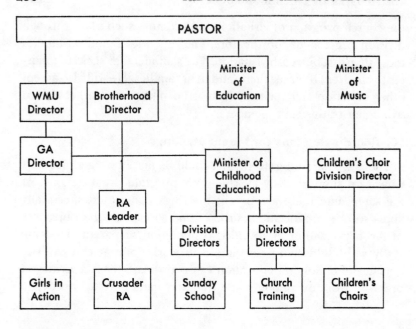

7.
The Minister of Preschool Education

The towering Empire State Building in New York City was for years the tallest structure in the world. Looming some 1,472 feet above the street level, its tower often stabs through the clouds with its impressive 102 stories. Yet, for all of the building's fame, it could never have risen to such astounding heights had there not been a carefully laid foundation. This incredible landmark rests upon Manhattan Island's solid rock strata, which rise to within a few feet of the ground's surface.[1]

Over two thousand years ago, Jesus spoke to his followers about the critical nature of foundations. Urging believers to be "wise like a man who builds his house on solid rock," Jesus reminded them that, "Though the rain comes in torrents, and the floods rise and the storm winds beat against his house, it won't collapse, for it is built upon rock" (Matt. 7:24–25, TLB).

From ancient days until now, the rule is the same. For any building to last and endure the processes of weathering, aging, and use, the greatest care must be given to laying a strong foundation. In the same way, the educational structure of any preschool ministry must rest upon firm foundations if lasting results are to be achieved.

I. THE MINISTER OF PRESCHOOL EDUCATION LAYS FOUNDATIONS

The minister of preschool education is the chief architect and construction engineer in laying foundations, too. But the marvel of his task is that his efforts are not directed toward lifeless structures, but rather toward living creations formed by the Master Planner's hand!

Little children, so pliable during the preschool years, are the recipients of the care, concern, and love of the minister of preschool education. This ministry is a profound endeavor in which the leader is literally one of the "labourers together with God" (1 Cor. 3:9). Creatively, he helps construct an atmosphere both at church and at home to encourage a foundation for spiritual growth.

Lifelong results come from efforts directed toward building (during the preschool years) foundations concerning God, Jesus, church, Bible, natural world, family, and others. The feelings and images that a child accumulates from birth to school age become the bedrock upon which the youngster's whole religious experience will be built.

Research supports the significance of learning in the preschool years. The December, 1971 issue of *Life* magazine presented overwhelming evidence that the ten-to-eighteen-month time span represents an individual's most crucial time of intellectual development. Dr. David Schrum in his book *Baby Care and Family Love* also affirms the fact that a child learns more in his first year of life than he does as a student in five years of college.[2]

The *Life* magazine article goes on to conclude that by the time a child is two, his mind-set and readiness for life are basically established. Further underscoring the significance of this second year, Dr. Edward Lindaman stated in a talk he presented to the Southern Baptist Planning and Promotion Commission that two years, seven months is the peak learning period in life. In his book *Stability and Change in Human Characteristics,* Benjamin Bloom suggests that by the time a child is four or five years of age, he has gained 50 percent of his total intelligence!

A broad array of evidence convincingly supports these staggering concepts. The significance of learning in the preschool years lends supreme importance to the role of the minister of preschool education.

Much of what a child's future life will be is akin to a blank billboard at birth. What he will someday become is difficult to imagine. But one thing is certain: A preschooler's life is richer and fuller when he and his family benefit from the support of the educational ministry of a church.

The profoundness of the fact that a church preschool program can dramatically shape a youngster's present and future lends impressive credibility to its ministry. Corrie ten Boom has voiced a vital truth in stating, "Young saplings are so much easier to bend than old tree trunks." [3] Consequently, the preschool program must move aggressively toward helping parents lay a meaningful foundation for spiritual growth in the life of every preschool child.

Obviously, the most productive, if not the best, time for laying foundations is in the preschool years. Even before birth, the minister of preschool education may begin to minister and lead others to minister to little children through the Cradle Roll department. And when the child is born, he may be brought into a church environment that is geared to the exciting task of building sound foundations for not only the preschool years but for all those years ahead.

II. The Minister of Preschool Education Stimulates Learning

In every area of life, if a person is to be effective, he must know *absolutely what he believes.* This fact means that ministers of preschool education must believe in certain fundamental truths. Three of these truths are basic in their importance:

First, preschool educators must function from the basic conviction that they are serving in response to Christ's call, "Suffer little children to come unto me, and forbid them not: for of such is the kingdom of God" (Luke 18:16).

Second, preschool educators must have a deep conviction about life and what Jesus had to say about it. "I came that they might have life, and that they might have it more abundantly" (John 10:10).

It is one thing to have life and quite another thing to *live* it! The ministry of preschool education provides countless opportunities to encourage abundant living. By investing time and concern, both in the lives of the preschooler and his parents, a preschool program enhances that family's opportunity to share the fullness of Christ-centered living!

Following Jesus' example, the minister of preschool education molds a pattern of ministry for preschoolers which underscores their infinite worth in their church and in their homes. Developing both a preschooler's sense of trust and his awareness of being loved are essential steps if the child is to grow spiritually.

While the understanding of Christ as a personal Savior is highly unlikely during these early years, each preschooler should have the opportunity to develop a progressive awareness of Jesus in ways appropriate to his level of development.

Third, preschool educators must believe that educational opportunities are life-centered. In the early years, meaningful learning is a result of life-centered experiences. In the Old Testament, God prescribed the pattern for teaching little children. Here is the life-centered concept: "O Israel, listen: Jehovah is our God, Jehovah alone. You must love him with all your heart, soul, and might. And you must think constantly about these commandments I am giving you today. You must teach them to your children and talk about them when you are at home or out for a walk; at bedtime and the first thing in the morning" (Deut. 6:4–7, TLB).

Practically stated, preschool education is essentially guiding the growth of preschoolers through natural teaching situations. It is through hearing, seeing, smelling, touching, and tasting that young children discover the wonders of God's world.

Preschool work in the church is no longer an aimless baby-sitting proposition. Laying spiritual foundations calls for the best in sensitivity, know-how, and teaching skill.

III. THE MINISTER OF PRESCHOOL EDUCATION CULTIVATES RELATIONSHIPS

Cultivating positive relationships must be the cornerstone of the structure for preschool ministry. Just as preschoolers learn about God's people by observing them in action, so relationships are a key to the success of the minister of preschool education. Four key groups require warm, loving, and supportive relationships.

The preschoolers.—Obviously, the child is the chief concern of the preschool educator. The needs, skills, and developmental levels of preschoolers suggest the approaches to be taken in teaching young boys and girls. Therefore, the program begins with the preschooler.

To serve preschoolers, the minister of preschool education must know them. Through careful and regular reading of a broad spectrum of preschool materials, one's knowledge of preschoolers expands. In addition, firsthand encounters with young children are essential to understanding preschoolers. In department settings, through visitation, and in incidental moments, the minister of preschool education gains a keen insight into the nature of these youngsters.

The workers.—Directors and teachers represent the heartbeat of the preschool ministry. Their dedication determines the temperature of the entire program. To shortchange a cultivative relationship with these workers is to hazard the ministry itself! Therefore, a teaching climate that establishes these leaders as ministers to preschoolers and their families must be built. The minister of preschool education must channel resources to the directors and teachers to equip them for their significant tasks.

Personal interaction with each worker must underscore the intrinsic worth and the distinct contributions that each teacher brings to the Preschool Division. In these direct contacts, it is good to utilize creative ways to say "thank you" and to repeatedly assure each worker that his role is of eternal importance.

Good relationships are supported in the following ways: (1) regular planning, (2) annual workers' retreats, (3) handwritten notes, (4) newsletter features, (5) personal ministry to worker needs, and (6) recognition of specific jobs well done. It is well to remember that the confidence of the workers in the minister of preschool education matures as frequent interactions cultivate these relationships.

As the minister of preschool education wisely utilizes time in planning sessions, the support of these meetings by the preschool workers grows. When they sense the director's unrelenting dedication to only the best in care, teaching, and ministry, they, too, become satisfied with only the loftiest standards. When the preschool educator actively acknowledges the ability of the workers to plan, execute, and evaluate various facets of the preschool program, he builds confidence in his leadership. In turn, the entire preschool ministry prospers.

The family.—No preschool program, however fine, is complete without a ministry to families with preschoolers. Even a quick comparison of the child's time at church versus his time at home underscores the urgent need for the church to support parents in their all-important task. Parents are, undeniably, a preschooler's most effective teacher.

These facts strongly assert that a progressive plan for family care giving must be established as an integral part of the preschool ministry. Churches must aggressively speak to the needs of families in today's world, and the best place to begin is in helping with their preschoolers. Care giving should include the following: (1) going into the homes, (2) cultivating caring relationships with parents, (3) reinforcing parents' efforts in child rearing through channeling resources such as the magazine *Living with Preschoolers,* take-home leaflets, cassettes such as *Our New Baby* and helpful books about preschoolers, and (4) providing frequent parent/worker meetings designed specifically to support homes. These actions are the minimal essential steps of ministry if preschoolers are to be nurtured in the Christian faith.

The church staff.—The minister of preschool education is not an island. This worker is as important as any other staff member.

It must be remembered, however, that the Preschool Division is only a part of the world. Its efforts must complement the total church ministry. Only through regular communication between staff members can these leaders give appropriate understanding, emphasis, and support to the ministry of the other staff people. Unquestionably, the love and respect shared among staff members cultivate that same love and respect across the entire spectrum of the church.

IV. THE MINISTER OF PRESCHOOL EDUCATION PROVIDES LEADERSHIP

Anything that grows must be nurtured. Leadership and followship are cases in point. The preschool workers look to the minister of preschool education for certain fundamental leadership functions. While in every church situation the ideal must be tempered with the real, the following are basic goals toward which the division leader must consistently strive.

1. The minister of preschool education assumes ultimate responsibility for every activity which falls under the preschool category, unless otherwise designated by the church. Alert not only to whether "things are OK," he guides workers toward the constant goal of developing that church experience into the most meaningful that it can possibly be.

2. The preschool educator is responsible for equipping the workers. This responsibility specifically calls for (1) scheduling regular planning sessions for the purpose of organizing and preparing for department teaching; (2) introducing workers to the latest in teaching methods and resources, including appropriate preschool study course books, supplementary resources, and other current materials relating to the developmental needs and abilities of preschoolers; and (3) promoting informative teacher-training conferences within his own church, association, state, and regional conference center.

3. The minister of preschool education works through the appropriate church channels in enlisting department workers. Key elements in enlistment include (1) seeking God's guidance through prayer; (2) creatively exploring solutions to leadership needs; and (3) scheduling a visit with the person one feels led to contact.

In the process of enlisting a worker, it helps to (1) explain why you feel that the person could effectively meet the teaching need; (2) invite the prospective worker to observe in a department setting;

(3) introduce the appropriate teaching guide used in the department; (4) leave a written list of the specific position responsibilities; (5) state specifically when a follow-up contact will be made to receive his prayerful answer. When the follow-up visit is made, graciously accept either a yes or a no. If the answer is yes, begin an immediate program of teacher training.

4. The minister of preschool education orders all of the necessary literature and supplies, in keeping with the requests of the workers and the policy of the church.

5. The minister of preschool education is ultimately responsible for the physical environment in each department.

6. The minister of preschool education has the privilege of communicating the program of the Preschool Division to the church family through a variety of creative means: bulletin board displays; articles in the church bulletin and/or the church paper; multimedia presentations in the worship service, with slides and script to highlight some aspects of the preschool ministry; and special promotions in Adult departments.

7. The minister of preschool education conducts a continuing program of family ministry to members and to prospects. For example, organizing a Cradle Roll department provides a unique opportunity to minister in homes where there are unchurched children below the age of two. Dividing department enrollees among department workers for quarterly visitation to deliver new literature ensures regular contacts with members. Extending help to families in special times of needs and joy reflects the church's care. Utilizing effective parent/worker meetings and fellowships fosters positive and open communication. Making maximum use of eye-catching mailings to support basic programs and philosophies highlights the church's concern for homes. Building a reservoir of books, cassette tapes, and filmstrips as resource helps to share through personal visitation and check-out programs increasingly prepares parents to guide growth of their preschoolers.

8. The minister of preschool education represents the Preschool Division on the church staff and church council planning.

V. The Minister of Preschool Education Exemplifies Growth

In laying firm foundations, the minister of preschool education must have a firm foundation of his own. Such a foundation springs from a pulsating faith and a daily walk with God. Yet there is more. Being a minister calls for several other basic growth activities:

1. A feeling of one's own identity and worth;
2. A deep conviction regarding the multiple joys in being one of God's people;
3. An interest in adult things aside from all that "walks and talks" preschool;
4. All of the formal education possible to prepare for the importance of the calling;
5. Solid grounding in the Southern Baptist preschool educational philosophy as reflected in the preschool study course books and various literature pieces;
6. A frequent exchange of ideas with other professionals through personal interactions, conferences, and seminars;
7. Continual immersion of oneself in the latest in preschool research and studies.

Above all, realizing that in order to be able to guide the lambs, it is essential to stay very near the Good Shepherd. "But seek ye first the kingdom of God, and his righteousness; and all these things shall be added unto you" (Matt. 6:33).

Notes

1. *Compton's Encyclopedia* 10 (1956), p. 217.
2. David Schrum, *Baby Care and Family Love* (Norwalk, Connecticut: C. R. Gibson Company, 1970), p. 17.
3. Corrie ten Boom, *Amazing Love* (Fort Washington, Pennsylvania: Christian Literature Crusade, 1953), p. 87.